The Overflow

i

The Overflow

An Outpouring of Prophetic Devotion

"You visit the earth and cause it to overflow; You greatly enrich it; The stream of God is full of water; You prepare their grain, for thus You prepare the earth."
Psalms 65:9

Doris M. Richardson

ISBN:978-0-578-58017-3

DBI Publishing, Inc.
Upper Marlboro, Maryland 20774

Holy Bible, King James Version: Public Domain

Scripture quotations identified (NKJV): Holy Bible, New King James Version. Copyright © 1979, 1980, 1983 by Thomas Nelson, Inc. Used by permission. All rights reserved.

Scripture quotations identified (NLT): Holy Bible, New Living Translation, Copyright © 1996. Used by permission of Tyndale Publishing House, Inc., Wheaton, Illinois 60189. Used by permission. All rights reserved.

Scripture quotations identified MSG: taken from The Message, copyright © 1993, 1994, 1995, 1996, 2000, 2001, and 2002 by Eugene H. Peterson. Used by permission of NavPress. Used by permission. All rights reserved. Represented by Tyndale House Publishers, Inc.

Scripture quotations identified (NIV): Holy Bible, New International Version, Copyright © 1973, 1978, 1984 by International Bible Society. Used by permission of Zondervan. Used by permission. All rights reserved.

Scripture quotations identified (TLB): The Living Bible, Copyright © 1971. Used by permission of Tyndale House Publishers, Inc., Carol Stream, Illinois 60188. Used by permission. All rights reserved.

Scripture quotations identified (NASB): New American Standard Bible, Copyright 1960, 1962, 1963, 1968, 1971, 1972, 1973, 1975, 1977. 1995 by The Lockman Foundation. Used by permission. All rights reserved.

Scripture quotations identified ESV® Bible: (The Holy Bible, English Standard Version®), copyright © 2001 by Crossway Bibles, a publishing

Dedication

This book is dedicated to my wonderful, loving, caring and protective husband, Calvin B. Richardson who has been a pillar of strength and inspiration for me through everything that I have endeavored to do. I could have done nothing without the comfort of knowing that my best friend and confidant was there to see me through the hurdles, difficulties and frustrations and to pick me up when I was down. He always reminded me that I can do all things through Jesus Christ who strengthens me.

Preface

I am honored that God would use me to share such rich and riveting messages with the Body of Christ in this final hour. I am sure you would agree that we are living in the most peculiar but yet amazingly profound time in the history of mankind. Many of us have never experienced such a time nor will we ever witness such a time again, in this life or the life to come. .

God spoke to me on September 17, 2003 and told me that the time of "The Gathering" has begun. I can only believe that there is an awesome mighty work to be accomplished in the Body of Christ and I would go so far as to say that we are the generation that God has chosen to live in this very extraordinary span of time as we know it and we are the instruments that He will use to "Gather" the end-time harvest.

To those who do not understand His divine plan and purpose, the significance of these times only casts a shadow from a very dim light, yet somehow it still holds a very disconcerting meaning. Conversely, to those of us who are "the called according to His purpose" (Romans 8:28), there is a profound realization that throughout the Scriptures, (both Old and New) there exists a period of extraordinary tribulation, in which the nature of God's wrath, judgment and divine indignation before the end-time glory has been repeatedly foreseen and foretold. This period is often referred to as the day of the Lord, a period in which God will come to "Gather" those of us who are His.

Many events will occur before that great and glorious day. In the meantime however, there is an enormous work for us to do. In order to perform in a manner fitting for a Royal Priesthood, a Chosen Generation" (1st Pet. 2:9). Surely these are trying and difficult times for many however, by the Grace of God, we have entered into another move of God victoriously, despite the enemy's attempts to take us out! We give God the Glory for His infinite Love that covers us day by day, moment by moment. So, as we move into another glorious year, please allow me to share with you these profound and timely messages from the Oracles of God that will encourage and bless you each day of the year, and for years to come.

Sunday, August 27, 2006
This is a time that I am bringing you into that you will serve me with all of your heart, mind, body and spirit. I am seeking those who would be unreservedly sold out to Me and Me alone. These are very crucial times and require those who would look beyond the comforts of life and lay down their lives for the gospel under any and all circumstances. The task is difficult, the reward is great.

Seek my Voice. I will tell you what is to come. I will show you the path that you must take to accomplish my will. My plan will unfold before you. I will make known to you the strategies that will be used to bring My people out of generations of bondage and deceit. They will be free to worship and serve Me in the true Spirit of Worship. I will restore Holiness to Zion. I will restore peace and I will heal hurts, wounds, diseases, feelings, minds, and relationships. I will also break down and destroy some things. I will remove the detestable things from among you. I will bring sons and daughters to a place where they will come to reverence the Christ in you more. They will begin to see you as priests in your households and respect the anointing on your lives. I will also bring this move upon your husbands and wives.

vii

Psalms 34:3
"O magnify the Lord with me, and let us exalt His name together."

Acknowledgements

First and foremost, I give honor, glory and praise to God Our Father, and to the Lord Jesus Christ, who filled me with the knowledge of Himself and an insatiable desire to understand His Word. I marvel at the level of trust that He has bestowed upon me, in that He has trusted me to convey His Word to His people. My greatest desire is simply to please Him. I also thank my husband Calvin, for every load of laundry, every trip to the grocery store, every meal from my favorite restaurant and for his reckless and unwavering love and support. He has enriched my life in so many ways and shown me what it means for a husband to "love his wife, as Christ loved the Church." When he was engaged in a blood-thirsty battle with the spirit of infirmity for his very life, his greatest concern was for me. That is love "unfeigned." Thanks to my daughter Renee for believing in me even when at times, I didn't believe in myself. To my sons Calvin Jr. and Derrick, who still think I am "the beautiful princess" who has grown up to be the "warrior queen," I love you. To the "Glory Girls" for making me feel that I am in a class all by myself. To Susannah, Christina, Shani and Chi, my beautiful daughters and armor bearers who are always on the wall and at the gates making intercession for me. I love you all. I also thank Apostle Deanna Vlijter (spiritual advisor and cherished friend), for her excellent example of Godliness, wisdom, knowledge and unwavering faith down through the years. To the countless unnamed giants, who have been pillars, light and salt for me

during my journey – thank you for your love and
encouragement.

x

Prologue

The Overflow Prophetic Devotional is an eclectic compilation of prophetic messages for the Body of Christ, poured out from the abundance of God's treasure of pure, cleansing, healing waters. It is intended expressly, to give life to our dry and thirsty hearts. To the reader, these riveting prophetic revelations will become an oasis; a wellspring of waters created by the power of the Later Rain, to pioneer and exemplify the return of the Spirit of Prophecy and Excellence in the Body of Christ. God has called us from the shadows and obscurities of this present age, to walk in the spiritual authority and power necessary to further establish God's Kingdom on the earth. We are called to lay down our lives, take up our weapons and assume our positions in the mighty army of the Lord; overcoming the temptations and seductions of the flesh and its nature (Romans 8:13). We will remain steadfast, immovable, these turbulent times! We will not be shaken in always abounding in the work of the Lord (1 Corinthians 15:58).

This powerful collection of God's Oracles, gives us a prophetic roadmap, which may be used to call us from a life of spiritual slumber to the awakening of a brand new dawning, as we await the "Mighty Overflow" anointing. This Spirit-ordained mighty awakening will cause a reverberating, profound and riveting awareness (of cataclysmic proportion), throughout the Nations; jolting the very core of our awareness, creating assurance of Victory from spiritual bondage! (1 Corinthians 15:57).

"Beloved, in My mercy I will yet send the living waters to wash away the stains created by sin and disobedience. To the faithful, I will cause you to walk in the "Overflow" of the previous "Outpouring," and upon you I will bestow the "double portion." John 7:38 (KJV)
He that believeth on me, as the scripture hath said, out of his belly shall flow rivers of living water.

Table of Contents

xiv

xv

The Overflow

Doris M. Richardson

The Overflow

Beloved, I have saturated you with My Spirit. I have poured out from the abundance of My treasure, pure, cleansing, healing waters upon your dry and thirsty land. I have made for you an oasis; a wellspring of waters created by the power of the Later Rain. I have washed you and cleansed you in this water, as I endeavored to also fill the cup of your longing with life sustaining springs of everlasting blessing. For it is I who daily supply you with the portion needed to sustain your soul.

I will now demonstrate what this mighty stream, created by My Spirit will do to prevent your souls from continuous suffering in a wilderness of problems, issues, despair, hopeless situations, needless pain, troubles, trials, tribulation, sickness, heartache and disease. I desire to demonstrate the outcome of your encounters with My Spirit. As I Released the Later Rain blessing in your midst, many came away fully drenched in the Rain of My Presence. Many are now carrying the seed that was watered abundantly in that previous demonstration. Yet some only experienced a mere dampening trickle and are in need of yet another opportunity to stand in that place, under the flow of My Spirit yet again, for you have once again become dry and parched.

Beloved, in My mercy I will yet send the living waters to wash away the stains created by sin and disobedience. To the faithful, I will cause you to walk in the "Overflow" of the previous

2

"Outpouring," and upon you I will bestow the "double portion." I have poured within you a wellspring which swells each time you lift a praise unto My name. I will release a perpetual wave of living waters into the deepest parts of your being, which will overflow and lift you higher with each expression of true praise and worship.

Others will be blessed as you lift your voice, raise your hands, and bow in reverence to Me. They will experience an "Overflow" anointing which will release them from many years of bondage and spiritual oppression. Many will experience My presence in this next wave. Step into the waters...walk in the "Overflow," says the Lord.

John 7:38 (KJV)
He that believeth on me, as the scripture hath said, out of his belly shall flow rivers of living water.

John 4:14 (KJV)
But whosoever drinketh of the water that I shall give him shall never thirst; but the water that I shall give him shall be in him a well of water springing up into everlasting life.

Exodus 23:25 (KJV)
And ye shall serve the Lord your God, and he shall bless thy bread, and thy water; and I will take sickness away from the midst of thee.

Doris M. Richardson

Rise Above Discouragement

Has it ever seemed that you were in a place where you were surrounded by the disparaging gloom of rejection, hurt and disappointment? Nothing that you do turns out right and those you love misunderstand even your greatest efforts to express your heart's cry? It is as if you were in a place where the only scenic view was a picture of dark clouds on the backdrop of a canvas of gloom. You try to breathe and with each gasping breath, your quivering lips manage to quietly whisper, "I'll be alright. Where is this undistinguishable place? How did I get here? I do not recognize anyone here though it is all strangely familiar." You fight to lift yourself out of this subterranean abyss, but somehow you know that you do not have the strength left to fight. Your spirit begins to cry out from the depths of your person, and you scuffle to break loose from the chains that bind your very soul and compete for your breath.

Beloved, it is time to cease from your struggles. The raging seas of time are drowning you in its perilous currents. There is no need to sink to the depths of discouragement that these currents bring. Do not lose sight of the power that formed the raging seas. Your adversary would have you to believe that it is only a destructive force that moves these currents along. But even in your discouragement My Creative Power to save exists.

You will not be destroyed nor utterly cast down, but you will rise above the currents of discouragement, destruction and defeat and ride upon the waves of restoration and creative ability. You will tread upon these waters as one who stands upon the Rock of Salvation. I am with you always.

2 Chronicles 20:17 (KJV)
Ye shall not need to fight in this battle: set yourselves, stand ye still, and see the salvation of the Lord with you, O Judah and Jerusalem: fear not, nor be dismayed; tomorrow go out against them: for the Lord will be with you.

2 Corinthians 12:9 (KJV)
And he said unto me, My grace is sufficient for thee: for my strength is made perfect in weakness. Most gladly therefore will I rather glory in my infirmities, that the power of Christ may rest upon me.

Hebrews 13:5 (KJV)
For he hath said, I will never leave thee, nor forsake thee.

Take Action

Beloved, I have spoken to you in times past regarding this current move of My Spirit in which I am pouring out My Spirit upon you to accomplish My Plan for mankind in this hour. This present outpouring will lift you to new levels of My Glory. I speak of a mighty anointing accompanied by My Grace, Mercy and Power to set the captives free and the release of those who have been locked within the confines of doubt and unbelief.

You must take action on previous prophecies and know that My Word shall accomplish what I have sent it to do. You are looking for Me to move according to what you have previously seen and heard, and what you think I will do. I tell you that I am constantly moving and shifting My power.

Take action to stand up and declare your faith in My Word. Raise your voice like an anthem and sing forth My praises. It is in the praise that I am moved to pour out My anointing like the oil that flowed down from Aaron's beard to the hem of his garment. Believe My Word that I have sent to you through My servants.

Move from the place of fear and intimidation that has literally frozen you for so long. Step out into the place of your Destiny and do not look back. How will you know where I truly desire you to be, unless you begin to take action and step into the place of your destiny by faith?

Continue to seek My Face in prayer with perpetual praise. I will stop the enemy in his tracks when you begin to take action. Do not sit still, shirk back, and cowl when you are called upon to praise Me. I cannot use you if fear grips you. Be bold, knowing that I have not given you the spirit of fear but rather of love, power, and a sound mind. Know that you must consecrate (sanctify, set apart) yourself for My service by much prayer and continual fasting.

I desire to release the power of My Anointing upon your life. Beloved, many are truly called, but few are Chosen. Know the signs of My Chosen Ones – the first sign is that of obedience; obedience calls for ACTION or an active state of mind, body and soul. Move out from your comfort zone. Step into the realm of the spirit. This requires you to act on My Word. Put your faith into action and become an active "Doer."

Leviticus 19:2 (KJV)
Speak unto all the congregation of the children of Israel, and say unto them, Ye shall be holy: for I the LORD your God am holy.

1 Peter 1:16 (KJV)
Because it is written, Be ye holy; for I am holy.

Doris M. Richardson

Do Not Be Moved By What You See

Beloved, the enemy has been extremely busy in this hour setting traps for you. He knows that you are still operating in the "sense" mode, believing what you see with the natural eye. When you function in this realm, it is impossible for you to discern and test the spirits. This makes it exceptionally easy for demon spirits to send strong delusions to you in the sense realm.

You must remember above all else, that you are not to be moved by what you see, hear, or feel in this realm. You are spirit and the "Greater One" lives in you. You must not give in to what you see in the natural when adversity comes your way, neither become sensitive to harsh and unwarranted accusation and lies. I tell you that I will contend with those who contend with you. I will take care of you. Do not be dismayed. Remember that everything in the world's system is temporary and will last only for a time.

Isaiah 11:3 (NIV)
And he will delight in the fear of the LORD. He will not judge by what he sees with his eyes, or decide by what he hears with his ears;

Isaiah 41:10 (KJV)
Fear thou not; for I am with thee: be not dismayed; for I am thy God: I will strengthen thee; yea, I will help thee; yea, I will uphold thee with the right hand of my righteousness.

8

Whose Voice Are You Hearing?

My children, are you hearing another voice? Does it seem that you are not receiving accurate directions? Are these voices transmitting messages that are contrary to My word? You must try the spirits Beloved, to see what type of messages they are sending to you. If what you are hearing seems contrary to prior truths written in My word, or to the prophecies that I have sent in order to bring you in line with My Divine Purpose for your life, then you are hearing "other voices."

These voices speak to you in the first person in an effort to entice you to believe that the thoughts that they impose upon you are actually a part of what you have received and rehearsed at some prior time. I speak to you in the second person Beloved, so that you may know and perceive that it is I. When I speak, you must clear the activities and chatter which takes place in your mind, as I speak to your spirit and your spirit transmits My words to your mind – your hearing.

My Spirit, which is within you, speaks to the deepest part of your inner being and you will receive immediate faith to believe My words which I speak through My Holy Spirit within you; "deep communicating with deep." It is in your spirit that My word is hidden and My Spirit will bring My word into your conscious thoughts, illuminating dark passages to the degree that you are able to understand them.

I long to communicate with you so that you may be well informed of how I am about to move in your situation, your surroundings and upon the face of the earth in this hour. I am issuing you a warning My Children. Just as the word of the Lord was precious in the days gone by, when I ceased from speaking to man because of the perverseness of his ways, so it will be even in these days because many choose to hear lying divinations which cause them to enter into sin and error. Only those who desire Me

Doris M. Richardson

above all else, will be able to hear My voice in the days ahead. Listen My Children, as you cannot afford to be on the battle field and not hear the clear warnings of the general. My sheep know My voice and I am known of mine. They will not follow the voice of a stranger. Listen and hear – your life depends upon it. You will be able to clearly distinguish. The Lord says, "Be still and know that I am God."

John 5:25 (KJV)
"Truly, truly, I say to you, an hour is coming and now is, when the dead will hear the voice of the Son of God, and those who hear will live."

Stay On Course

Beloved, did you not know that you have been called to tread upon serpents and scorpions? You must stay on course and not allow the things around you to obscure your vision. Yes, I know that there have been many disappointments. But these come only for your strengthening and to sharpen your insight. A Divine appointment comes with many disappointments, but be aware that these disappointments are spawned out of a natural desire to accomplish My will (which is spiritual), by earthly means. Dear ones, this is the only thing which is <u>impossible</u> to you. I have equipped you with spiritual weaponry and armor so that you may go forth (in the natural) and execute My sovereign plan (which is spiritual). You cannot accomplish my will by use of your intellect or reasoning.

No, you may not always understand My techniques and strategies, for they are not created or engineered by the reasoning capabilities of mere man. My ways are not your ways...and neither are My thoughts your thoughts. Because you are measuring the tasks that are set before you by physical means, you have allowed the enemy to cause you to go off course.

The task cannot be accomplished by your tactics. There are no human metrics by which you may measure the success of them. You have been called to "build" My church – my body. However, before a builder proceeds, he must first count up the cost.

Beloved, building buildings and structures of that kind is much easier than building people. Yes, it is very difficult to build people, as there may be times when the very ones that you nurture and grow turn their backs on you; and many even set their hearts against you. I tell you that for this, your reward is great in heaven. But in order to build My people, you yourself must be strong and stay close to Me. I will show you how to be successful; for this desire comes from Me. It is not a natural desire.

Stay on course, even in the face of disappointment. I have called you to be a "trailblazer." Keep this ever before you. Stay the course. The "easy" course was not chartered by My Spirit. You have chosen the "straight and narrow" road. I did not tell you that there would not be obstacles on this road. This road was constructed to allow very little room for deviation. To do so, you must "turn back." Do not put your hand to the plow and turn back.

Stay before Me in prayer. For only I, can remove the stumbling blocks and obstacles from your path. For with one mighty blast from My Breath (Ruach Ha-Kadesh), I can send a wind of change which will turn the course of events, and you shall be successful in every appointment. Stay On Course.

Luke 9:62 (KJV)
And Jesus said unto him, No man, having put his hand to the plough, and looking back, is fit for the kingdom of God.

Deuteronomy 8:19 (KJV)
And it shall be, if thou do at all forget the Lord thy God, and walk after other gods, and serve them, and worship them, I testify against you this day that ye shall surely perish.

Storms Are Surfacing

Set in order those things which are in disarray. Pluck up, tear down, then rebuild and restore the remains. Rearrangement is needed for the success of your plan, but some things are not in the right order. Things are beginning to experience a great positional upheaval. This upheaval has begun on the inside and will affect a tremendous outward change.

A cleansing has begun and this cleansing will continue until all underlying layers of filth (sin) and uncleanness have been brought to the surface and eradicated. Storms are surfacing. These storms are brought about by the issues of life. These storms will cause floods which will affect rising waters and cause them to emerge. These will be cleansing waters which will cause all inner filth (sin) to rise to the surface and be discarded, washed away and eliminated.

Take heed of all that has been given to you. Satan has begun to attack and cause disharmony and disunity among you. You will not be able to withstand these attacks unless you build a united front, a strong tower against the storms. You must come together; fast and pray. Then and only then will you be able to defeat and disarm the enemy. Do not be disturbed or disheartened by what you see. This activity occurred to divert your attention from the real source of the attack.

The purpose of this present attack is to cause a division among you. You shall emerge from this attack stronger, and more unified when you pray, fast, repent and forgive. Then I will move on your behalf to cause all opposition to cease.

Psalm 46:10
"Be still, and know that I am God. I will be exalted among the nations, I will be exalted in the earth!"

Doris M. Richardson

Exodus 14:14
The LORD will fight for you; you need only to be still."

14

A Time of Refreshing - The Outpouring

I am your shield from the desert sun, your oasis and a well-spring of cool, still waters to satisfy your dry and parched land. I am bringing forth a time of refreshing and you will be revived in the cool, flowing waters from heaven. You will be refreshed and refilled. You have only to rest in Me and receive during this great outpouring of My refreshing waters, says the Lord.

You have given so much and now it is time for the return on your investment. Open your hearts and receive, and you will experience a greater outpouring of My Spirit. You will regain the sum of your confidence My children, which the enemy has been striving to steal from you. You have held fast against many odds and you have not forgotten, but held fast to the confidence that you have in Me. Now, I will demonstrate My love for you in a tangible and overt manner, so that the world may marvel and be amazed.

You have experienced many dark days; fightings and fears within and without. You have been tossed and driven by the winds of adversity, but yet you held fast to My name. There were great tremors in the heavenlies that reverberated even to the netherworld, each time you cried out and called My name. Now you will call My name yet again and it shall take on a new meaning for you. Your spirit will be quieted within you when you utter My name. Peace shall enter into your dwelling, when you call My name. Demons will tremble and be compelled to restore all that they have stolen from you, when you call My name with confidence and assurance.

This is the Time of Refreshing and Restoration. My children step into this moment and regain your momentum. Then rejoice and offer a Shabach! To the Lion of Judah, who brought you out of the wilderness? Offer a Judah praise to the Lord of Lords and the King of Kings. Rejoice!

Doris M. Richardson

Proverbs 1:23 (KJV)
Turn you at my reproof: behold, I will pour out my spirit unto you, I will make known my words unto you.

Acts 2:17 – 18 (KJV)
¹⁷And it shall come to pass in the last days, saith God, I will pour out of my Spirit upon all flesh: and your sons and your daughters shall prophesy, and your young men shall see visions, and your old men shall dream dreams:
¹⁸And on my servants and on my handmaidens I will pour out in those days of my Spirit; and they shall prophesy:

Acts 10:45 (KJV)
And they of the circumcision which believed were astonished, as many as came with Peter, because that on the Gentiles also was poured out the gift of the Holy Ghost.

It Is Time

It is time for My people to truly know and experience the depths of My Love. I have poured out My love upon you in times past and have washed you with the water of My Word. You have benefited greatly from the blessings that have been poured out and showered down upon you, as you stepped under the fountains of My Love when you were in need of a healing – a cleansing of your souls. But I tell you that the Outpouring that you are about to experience will be incomparable to that of past distributions.

You will begin to experience a Great and Mighty Release of My power that will send the world around you into a whirlwind. Many will begin to step out in the calling and giftings of My Spirit, which will be so powerful that it will rock and shatter the very existence of demonic world forces. Chains will be loosed and those in captivity will be set free from years of bondage and fear. No longer will My people cowl and fear at the sound of the tempest.

There will be a mighty clamoring sound apparent in the netherworld, as the prayers of My people jar (shake, shock and vibrate) prison doors and cause them to swing open, so that the captives may walk through with ease. There will be a mighty shout like unto the shout heard around the Jericho walls when they caved in, as the cries of My servants were heard. It will be a cry of Unity in the Spirit. A shout of Victory and Praise! I will set those free who have been chained in the prison of mind control, mental illness, emotional bondage, fear and trepidation. I will release many from the prison of poverty and lack.

I will restore harmony and peace, among My people and establish the fortified cities which will be built upon the foundations of love, joy, and peace. I will give new hope to My people. It is Time!

Romans 8:38-39 (NIV)
For I am convinced that neither death nor life, neither angels nor demons, neither the present nor the future, nor any powers, neither height nor depth, nor anything else in all creation, will be able to separate us from the love of God that is in Christ Jesus our Lord.

A New Day

Dear Ones, this is a new day and you are entering into a new order of things. Did I not tell you that the old things have passed away? This new day will herald (proclaim; announce; publish) a new moving of My Spirit, says the Lord. I am shifting the order of things in your life.

No longer will you serve Me from the distance. Yes, now you will emerge, for I am calling you forth. You can no longer hide in your insecurities. I am rebuilding the ancient ruins and bringing forth a day of deliverance, a day of joy and rejoicing.

Do not gaze upon the world's situations for I am building for you new heavens and a new earth. I am preparing those who desire to step out of themselves, lay down the shroud that binds them and purpose themselves to step into this new era, this new level, this new plateau.

Dare to believe in spite of what you see. Become radical in your belief and the execution of your belief. Burst forth My children with a mighty explosion of the creative power which resides within you even now. Search for it just as you would a lost treasure, for it is valuable, even priceless. You will need this mighty power as I send you forth to bring faith and deliverance to those who are imprisoned by tradition, religion, and world order.

I tell you that there is no order on this earth. Men cry out for peace but it shall not come until the Prince of Peace returns. Until then, continue working to restore the ancient ruins – Zion will be restored.

Doris M. Richardson

Joel 2:25-26 (KJV)
And I will restore to you the years that the locust hath eaten, the cankerworm, and the caterpillar, and the palmerworm, my great army which I sent among you.Jeremiah 30:18-22 (NKJV) "Thus says the LORD, 'Behold, I will restore the fortunes of the tents of Jacob and have compassion on his dwelling places; And the city will be rebuilt on its ruin, And the palace will stand on its rightful place. 'From them will proceed thanksgiving and the voice of those who celebrate; And I will multiply them and they will not be diminished; I will also honor them and they will not be insignificant. 'Their children also will be as formerly, And their congregation shall be established before Me; And I will punish all their oppressors.

The Unchartered Course

Ask Me and I will open your spiritual eyes and give you sharper visual acuity in the spirit realm. You will begin to see clearly, the devices and schemes used to divert your focus from the eternal to the temporal. You will be lifted up out of the dark abyss of spiritual blindness and begin to see into the "now" as well as the "future." You will know how to plan ahead and strategize in order to prepare for your divine calling.

I am calling those into ministry in this hour who will be willing to step out into a place unseen. To launch out into a course unchartered, to trust me to provide all things. I will fulfill My promises. I will bring you to a new plateau, a place of perpetual praise. For it is in the praise that you will experience and see great wonders as I draw closer to you. I will shower you with strength to overcome. You will experience a deeper sense of My Divine Presence and Provision.

I am the God who is More Than Enough. Why do you suffer lack? Search for Me. I am so close. My word is near to you; even in your mouth. You have only to speak forth the words that I have spoken to you and see them take on life. Do not look at the situation to believe it. Believe it not; unless I have proclaimed it. Decree your position and make a covenant with Me that it may come to pass. Speak the word. You shall decree a thing and it shall be so.

Walk uprightly before Me and keep My commandments. I am with you. Look into the spirit realm and you will see Me. For yes, you have seen Me already. Believe what you see in the spirit as I open your eyes.

Genesis 12:1-3 (KJV)
Now the Lord had said unto Abram, Get thee out of thy country, and from thy kindred, and from thy father's house, unto a land

that I will shew thee: ² *And I will make of thee a great nation, andI will bless thee, and make thy name great; and thou shalt be a blessing:*

³ *And I will bless them that bless thee, and curse him that curseth thee: and in thee shall all families of the earth be blessed.*

The End Justifies the Means

Beloved, you have not experienced the pain of the Cross. You have not partaken of the Cup that I drank of, nor have your sufferings come near to that which I had to endure. Little Ones, have I not said, "think it not strange the fiery trials that are to try you?" Have I not said that, "with every temptation I will make a way of escape for you, so that you may be able to bear it?"

You have endured a season of great trials but I tell you that "The End Justifies the Means." You will see and believe that every trial you have been through has elevated you to another level of strength and endurance. I have given you the power to overcome obstacles and rise above spiritual stagnancy.

Many have desired to reach higher plateaus, climb spiritual mountain tops, and reach deeper depths of worship. I tell you that in order to ascend, it is necessary that you complete the phase that you are currently experiencing.

Where were you when I was in the Garden pleading to the Father to "remove this cup?" If it was necessary that I should drink from the cup in order to accomplish salvation for the world, then the servant is no greater than his Master. Did you not know that you are seated together with Me at the right hand of the Father? My Dearly Beloved, I have given you the keys that will open the doors of Faith to believe that Satan is under your feet and all things are possible for you.

Do not linger in yesterday's trials. This is the season of New Beginnings. Yes, you will face greater, but fewer trials this year. You are fully prepared.

James 1:2-4 (ESV)
Count it all joy, my brothers, when you meet trials of various kinds, for you know that the testing of your faith produces

steadfastness. And let steadfastness have its full effect, that you may be perfect and complete, lacking in nothing.

Romans 5:3-4 (RSV)
More than that, we rejoice in our sufferings, knowing that suffering produces endurance, and endurance produces character, and character produces hope.

I Am Building

Beloved, I am still building My Church and the gates of Hell shall not prevail against it. My people shall not be devoured by the spirits of darkness. I will protect those who belong to me.

Remember My apostles? My Father gave them to Me that they may carry on My works in the earth realm. I protected them from evil and from the evil one and none were lost, except Judas Iscariot, the Son of Perdition. Satan has come to sift many of you like wheat but he shall not prevail.

I have set you apart unto Myself and I will preserve you for the working of My will, until the Gospel has been preached to all nations and creeds. I am building character in you that you may be strong and courageous for the battle. I am building Faith in you so that you may believe that all things are possible. You will begin to demonstrate the effectiveness of the words that I have spoken concerning My saints.

You will begin to speak creatively to every situation, circumstance, obstacle and hindrance, commanding these demon forces to cease from their maneuvers and attacks against My people. You will begin by faith, to speak creatively to dead parts and they shall live.

New life shall result when you call into existence, the mighty forces of My power into your everyday circumstances. You shall decree a thing and I shall move to make it so. Have I not told you that "the word of God is near you, even in your mouth?" I am building in you integrity so that you may gain the honor and respect that is becoming for a man or woman of God in this hour. That the people may indeed say, "we will follow you, for we perceive that God is with you."

I am building in you trustworthiness, temperance, goodness, longsuffering, love, joy, peace, meekness, and power so that your fruit may remain. I will speak to you often and you will begin to have the courage and boldness to proclaim My words that I will speak to you.

I will teach you how to build up those around you who have been down trodden, depressed and defeated for so long. Yes, I am still building so that all pieces are jointly fitted together in the building that I am constructing.

Matthew 16:18 (KJV)
And I say also unto thee, That thou art Peter, and upon this rock I will build my church; and the gates of hell shall not prevail against it.

Bitterness and Unforgiveness Must Go!

Beloved, you need to let go of unforgiveness because it is weighing you down like a ball and chain. This is just another attack of the enemy of your soul. You must resist him! Do not allow your past to hold you prisoner. Break loose, break free from the shackles of hurts and wounds that you have become all too familiar with. Do not carry guilt for the decisions that you have made in the past. Those things have been placed in the sea of forgetfulness so you must move on. This is the time of the open door and you must situate yourself to move through those new doors. Go ahead and make that decision to move on because to not move forward at this time would be a travesty.

I tell you to break loose My child. With the power that exists within you, free yourself from the entanglement of bitterness and never allow it to sink into your mind and soul again. You will find that you will begin to feel lighter when the false burdens are lifted. I have not called you into this. My will for you is that you be free so that you may continue along the path to your destiny. Leave the past behind and press on with new hope. Hope deferred makes the heart sick. Beloved, you know all too well what you must do, but you hold back for fear of offending.

Use the keen spiritual gifts and insight that I have given you, so that you may indeed see through My eyes what needs to be done in this hour. Open your spiritual eyes seer and peer into the course that I have set before you. This is not the time to allow the spirit of bitterness which works through those who are without, to choke life from you for fear of offending. The kingdom of God suffers violence and the violent must forcefully take possession of it. Stand in your rightful place and fight. Do not lay down, kowtow or relinquish the reigns. Hold on. Take what is yours by force! It is your inheritance. You are in control. Let that which does not edify and bring peace into your life move on– let it go! Spirits of Bitterness are most often identifiable by their explicit functions (such as):

Keeping hurtful incidents alive – things that happened years ago, are as fresh and alive as they were the very day when they first occurred.

The individual is carrying the double load of dealing with current problems and as well as an accumulation of past hurts and wounds. The Spirit of Unforgiveness keeps every detail of the hurts alive in the very forefront of your mind and incessantly replays them ad nauseam, day after day.

Despite continual confession of forgiveness, the most insignificant hurt is neither forgiven, nor forgotten. Wherever the attitude of bitterness is found, the following demon groupings will most likely be present and manifest:

Resentment
Hatred
Unforgiveness
Violence
Temper
Anger
Retaliation
Murder
Continual prayer and fasting is the only solution for deliverance from this dreadful spirit.

Matthew 17:21 (NASB)
"But this kind does not go out except by prayer and fasting."

Take It to the Lord in Prayer

Dear Ones, I am here to comfort, console and guide you. I am your burden bearer, your decision maker, your life-force, your source, your protection, your strong tower, and your defense. Before the day was formed, I am He. You must come to Me so that I can work it all out for you. You look for answers in the wrong places. No one can be for you what I am. Turn to Me. I am the one who created you. Yes, the one who creates good and evil, light and darkness.

I was with you in the doctor's office when you chose to believe the medical reports. But Beloved, I was wounded for your transgressions and bruised for your iniquities. The punishment for your peace was upon Me and by My stripes you were healed.

Now whose report will you believe? I was with you when the tears welled up in your eyes as you lay quietly upon your pillow in the night watch with tears rolling down your cheeks like raindrops on your pillow. Ah My child, take comfort in knowing that I was there and I dried your tears until you fell asleep in the night watch.

Did you not know that weeping only endures for the night season, but joy comes in the morning? Do not forget that I am with you at all times. I looked for you during the 4th watch but though your spirit was willing, your flesh was hindered by the spirit of slumber. My child, it is essential that you rest. You cannot be an effective intercessor if your body is tired. Apply wisdom in your daily activities, and remember that I never require more of you than you are able to produce. Moreover, it is I who gives you strength to endure. Remember, My strength is perfected in your weakness.

I desire so much more for you. I have plans for your life. Yes, great plans. But you cannot bear the burdens imposed upon you by giving place to unclean spirits who seek only to destroy, even bring you to an early grave. Do not depend upon the arms of flesh. I alone am He who is able to deliver you. Prayer is essential Beloved. For it is during these times when your spirit communes with Me, that you are given instructions unique to your situation and refreshing waters flood your thirsty soul. For My Spirit intercedes for you with groanings that cannot be spoken in your natural language. You speak mysteries by My Spirit, for the healing of the nations. Bring it to Me in prayer, says the Lord.

Philippians 4:6 (NKJV)
Do not be anxious about anything, but in everything by prayer and supplication with thanksgiving let your requests be made known to God.

Colossians 4:2 (ESV)
Continue steadfastly in prayer, being watchful in it with thanksgiving.

Drowning in the Desert

Beloved, you are in the middle of a desert and yet you are drowning. "How can this be?" you say. "Great swelling waves are overtaking me so that I can not breathe. I can hear the gurgling sound of the water as I struggle to take my last breath," you say. But I tell you that the gurgling sounds are the sounds of the waters of life which are emerging from the eternal well of the River of Life within you.

You are being washed and cleansed by the eternal power of My Spirit as I prepare you for ministry. This ministry requires that you linger a while in the dry places on the back side of the desert; in a place where the land appears to be dry and parched from the penetrating heat of the sun. For it is in this place that I will prepare you for the great deluge (downpour) of the later rain upon your dry and thirsty soul.

It is here that you will learn the significant meaning of the River of Life which flows through you; that wellspring which emerges into life eternal. The water is graceful and vibrant. It is powerful and has life and motion. It will cause you to show forth My praise to the nations – to generations!

Isaiah 41:18 (NIV)
I will make rivers flow on barren heights, and springs within the valleys. I will turn the desert into pools of water, and the parched ground into springs.

Do Not Doubt Your Calling

The gifts and calling that I have birthed within you are genuine. Do not doubt your calling. Do not waiver, fold, or shirk back. For though you measure yourself by your own feelings, know that My Spirit does not flow through you by your own volition or desires. Many have longed to experience what you are now experiencing, but this special anointing does not come from the will of man.

I have lifted and elevated you to a new place; a place in which you can only arrive as you ascend to new plateaus in the spirit realm. You will find that in this place, you will begin to notice (with heightened awareness), that the things which you have desired so earnestly in the spirit are suddenly becoming more real to you. You will discern things which were once vague and obscured, with greater acuity and precision.

You will begin to prophecy openly with greater fluency and accuracy. You will begin to experience more open visions as well as dreams. As you yield to My calling without hesitation, you will indeed soar in the spirit and gain strength to proclaim My Word to the multitudes, the nations.

Fire will proceed from your mouth and consume that which is sinful and wicked and purify that which remains. Seek Me. Run to Me. I have called you to build up people who have been down trodden and forgotten. You will share My Word with them; which will feed their hungry souls and give drink to their dry and parched lands; that they may bring forth a harvest of abundant life; that they may live again in this hour.

Romans 11:29 (KJV)
For the gifts and calling of God are without repentance.

Psalms 91:15 (KJV)
He shall call upon me, and I will answer him: I will be with him in trouble; I will deliver him, and honor him.

Doris M. Richardson

Emergent Urgency

My child, seek Me with your whole heart. I am waiting for you to draw near. I will show you what your urgency should really be. You have suffered and survived an insurmountable attack against your emotions, even your will. You have become tired and are experiencing feelings of defeat, all because during your emergent times of embattlement you did not seek Me, but rather turned to other sources to seek answers. You said that I did not answer when you called. My child, but I did. Your urgency in this hour is not your problem, or the battle that you are currently engaged in, but rather it is the feeling of abandonment that engulfs you because of your turning away from me. So, turn to me and seek forgiveness and I will order your steps accurately and set you on the right path. For your urgency will no longer emerge and bring you to a place of loneliness and despair, because in My presence there is fullness of joy. Remember My Child that I am always with you and you can depend on the safety of My love.

2 Chronicles 7:14 (KJV)
14 If my people, which are called by my name, shall humble themselves, and pray, and seek my face, and turn from their wicked ways; then will I hear from heaven, and will forgive their sin, and will heal their land.

Sharpen Your Sword – There Is War Ahead

Beloved, the days ahead will be filled with demonic activity of great proportions. The people of the earth will be visited by demonic forces of enormous strength. Their sting will penetrate deeply within the souls of those who have been weakened by the formation of resilient alliances, with their blood-thirsty desire to cripple and thwart the work of My hands within the earth. The weapons of your warfare indeed are not carnal, but mighty through the working of My Spirit. My Word of Truth will be the deadliest weapon against these forces. My Word is Tested, Tried and sure to be your greatest defense.

I have given you the power to speak creatively to the netherworld; commanding them to adhere to the Living Word of God; the Word that transcends time and space; the Word so powerful that life is created when it is spoken. The word that reverberates and the earth quakes; oceans move to form powerful currents that destroy even the surface of the earth; trees are plucked up by their roots and mountains reduced to ashes. I have told you to study My word so that you will be able to stand strong and proclaim to the world that you are My servant, My Commander, My General who with one blast of the tongue can destroy enemy armies, reducing them to nothing.

This is the time of War! The time that I have been preparing you for many years now. I have protected you from the destructive onslaught that the devil and his angels have schemed against you even from the days of your youth. He desired to steal the weapon of Worship from you, but I hid your worship and protected it, because it was a habitation even to Me. Through your weapon of worship, many were protected and set free from bondage, deception, weakness, fear, deceit, and despair. The Word of My power is hidden deeply within you and has enlarged in power and greatness. In fact, it is so great that Satan and his demons even fear, what you might proclaim against them. Fast, pray at all times and you will be cleansed with the washing of water by the Word. My Word is Alive and Powerful! Sharpen your Sword, says the Lord.

Ephesians 5:26-27 (KJV)
26 That he might sanctify and cleanse it with the washing of water by the word,
27 That he might present it to himself a glorious church, not having spot, or wrinkle, or any such thing; but that it should be holy and without blemish.

Deuteronomy 32:41 (ESV)
If I sharpen My flashing sword, And My hand takes hold on justice, I will render vengeance on My adversaries, And I will repay those who hate Me.

Learn To Love

Dear Ones, I am saddened when I see that you still have not learned how to love, nor have you learned the meaning of "Agape." What does it profit you to love those with whom you are familiar and a stranger you will not receive? Love causes you to look above "SEE" level and brings you into the realm of the Spirit. You must learn to love those who are not so lovely to behold outwardly; those who are scorned and looked down upon by society because of their social status, for I am sending those who need to experience "unfeigned" love. Those who were not afforded the same opportunities as you – the unlovely.

Did I not tell you that you must not forget to entertain strangers for in so doing, you may be entertaining angels unknowingly? Remember that you were vile and filthy when you came to Me and I received you with open arms. Sin had disfigured you and marred your beauty, but I embraced you and poured My love upon you. I took your scarred and disfigured vessel and created a vessel of honor. I washed and cleansed you with My blood and then I arrayed you with beauty. There is no Greater Love and no greater commandment. Learn to Love – begin in your household. Many must learn to love the members of their own households before their love becomes far-reaching, even able to defy all bounds. My love for you is boundless.

The Greatest Commandment:

Mark 12:28-31 (NIV)
One of the teachers of the law came and heard them debating. Noticing that Jesus had given them a good answer, he asked him, "Of all the commandments, which is the most important?"
"The most important one" answered Jesus, is this: "Hear, O Israel, the Lord our God, the Lord is one. Love the Lord your God with all your heart, and with all your soul, and with all your mind, and with all your strength." The second is this:

37

Doris M. Richardson

"Love your neighbor as yourself. There is no commandment greater than these."

Wait For My Leading

Dearly beloved, during this hour it is imperative that you wait for My leading before making any major decisions. You must clearly distinguish between My voice and the voice of your human spirit. These are very difficult to distinguish at times and every difficult decision requires time and precision. You must know precisely how you must move.

Do not be quick to seek counsel from those who are riding the waves of chaos even in their own personal situations. Seek wise counsel; seek My face for the solutions to your problems and dilemmas. For surely My counsel shall stand and I will not disappoint.

I am seeking those in this hour who will hear the voice of the Spirit and be confident and sure that I am calling "deep to deep." The place that you are standing in My Beloved, is the place to which I have called you in order to accomplish My purposes for your life.

Be careful that you do not miss this opportunity to become My voice and My hands in this hour. I will use you to lead many who are treading dark paths trying to find My Glorious Light. But first, you must turn your ear to Me and strive to hear My voice even among the clamor of many other voices. Believe that it is My desire that you become well-acquainted with the very "Light of Men" so that you may continue along the path that I have set for you and so that you may re-direct My people. It is My desire that they experience My deep and abiding love for them. As My voice, you will tell them to "quiet their souls" that they may truly hear My voice. For My sheep know My voice. Tell My people to "be still and know that I Am God," and I will lead them into truth. Be still and wait for My leading.

Psalm 27:14 (KJV)
Wait on the LORD: be of good courage, and he shall strengthen thine heart: wait, I say, on the LORD.

Section 2

The Outpouring

The Spirit Of "More" Is Sweeping the Universe

Beloved, the hearts of My people (who really love Me), are crying out for "More" of Me. More faith, obedience, anointing, grace, love, power, faith, wisdom, understanding and reverence which can only come through a release of My Spirit and a deep, deep longing. My Spirit is at work sweeping across the face of the universe, dispersing, dispensing and gathering that which is mine. Not even one particle of matter will be displaced (left under foot) at the end of this miraculous process. I am shaking, sweeping and gathering in this hour, those whose hearts are longing for the seed of my anointing and My Grace for "More."

My capacity to fill My people with more love, grace, faith, and joy is unsearchable and endless. For you see beloved, it has been given to some, the capacity to receive even "More" of Me. I am sweeping, dispersing and releasing "More" of My Spirit into the atmosphere in this hour and many have been blessed with the capacity to grasp, store and accommodate this unusual distribution. This powerful and mighty sweeping shall result in an outpouring of My Spirit; the likes of which has never been known.

Healing for the nations will be swept up in the heap of this great move; incurable diseases will suddenly be eradicated. Many will be set free from conditions brought about by curses and incantations sent forth by evil spirits and workers of wickedness of varying categories and groupings.

Organs and limbs shall regrow through the miraculous working of cellular regeneration and the Word of My Spirit; for you are fearfully and wonderfully made. I will cause an ability for panoramic vision and insight to come upon your natural capacity to see in the earth realm, and you will begin to supernaturally see with precision, what heaven sees. I will place upon you an extraordinary "knowing," or a supernatural capacity to discern and glean with the wisdom and insight that heaven deems ordinary. These things will I do for those who yet desire "More" of Me, says the Lord.

Psalm 92:13-14 (NIV)
¹² The righteous will flourish like a palm tree, they will grow like a cedar of Lebanon; ¹³ planted in the house of the LORD, they will flourish in the courts of our God. ¹⁴ They will still bear fruit in old age, they will stay fresh and green,

Hebrews 6:1 (NIV)
¹ Therefore let us move beyond the elementary teachings about Christ and be taken forward to maturity, not laying again the foundation of repentance from acts that lead to death, and of faith in God,

2 Peter 3:18 (NIV)
¹⁸ But grow in the grace and knowledge of our Lord and Savior Jesus Christ. To him be glory both now and forever! Amen.

Break Loose

Dear Ones, it is time to cease from your struggles. The raging seas of time are drowning you in its perilous currents. There is no need to sink to the depths of discouragement that these currents bring. Do not lose sight of the power that formed the raging seas. Your adversary would have you to believe that it is only a destructive force that moves these currents along. But even in your discouragement My Creative Power to save exists.

You will not be destroyed nor utterly cast down, but you will rise above the currents of discouragement; destruction and defeat and ride upon the waves of restoration, creative ability, and walk or tread upon these waters as one who stands upon the Rock of Salvation.

Joshua 1:3-6, 9 (KJV)
3 Every place that the sole of your foot shall tread upon, that have I given unto you, as I said unto Moses.
4 From the wilderness and this Lebanon even unto the great river, the river Euphrates, all the land of the Hittites, and unto the great sea toward the going down of the sun, shall be your coast.
5 There shall not any man be able to stand before thee all the days of thy life: as I was with Moses, so I will be with thee: I will not fail thee, nor forsake thee.
6 Be strong and of a good courage: for unto this people shalt thou divide for an inheritance the land, which I sware unto their fathers to give them. 9 Have not I commanded thee? Be strong and of a good courage; be not afraid, neither be thou dismayed: for the Lord thy God is with thee whithersoever thou goest?

The Gathering

The time of the "Gathering" has begun. I am gathering My people from the north, south, east and west. I am gathering My harvest. I have shaken, I have torn down, I have plucked up and I have rebuilt. I have blown My wind, My mighty wind upon the earth realm and now it is time for gathering up that which could not be shaken, that which still stands, that part which remains steadfast and immovable.

I am calling for a mighty army who will not be afraid to step out in this hour to preach the gospel of the gathering. An army which is undaunted by the move of the church today; which will not be afraid to stand against the lies of the whore, the great whore Babylon. An army that will not be afraid to stand up and proclaim that sin is rampant in the church. Greed has become the essential theme, while salvation and repentance has long since been pushed aside.

I have watched My people suffer. I have seen the devastating effects on their souls. I have seen the creature worshipped in the sanctuaries. I have observed as the hearts of men were turned in deceit, while the larger issues are not dealt with. I am tired of greedy preachers preying upon My people. No, this is not a pleasant word and many will not want to listen. But the remnant that I am gathering will hear and believe that it is I.

I will protect My people during the perilous times that are to come. I will instruct and inform them how to survive these tines. I am sending many sure disasters upon the earth realm, but the end is yet to come. My people will be My voice during these times. I will impart My words unto them. There will be healing for the nations in My words that I will impart to them. I will sanctify, yes, I will purify that which is mine. I will prepare my saints to reign with Me. I am gathering those whose garments are untainted by the perverseness of this wicked generation. I

45

have spoken, I have pled, I have sent My prophets, I have sent My Son, I have sent peril and famine, and flood. But look, it is time now that I must come and I come with fire; for I am an All-Consuming Fire. I will purify and I will destroy. Know that it is I – for I Am God.

Malachi 3:1-3, 6 (KJV)
¹ Behold, I will send my messenger, and he shall prepare the way before me: and the Lord, whom ye seek, shall suddenly come to his temple, even the messenger of the covenant, whom ye delight in: behold, he shall come, saith the Lord of hosts.
² But who may abide the day of his coming? and who shall stand when he appeareth? for he is like a refiner's fire, and like fullers' soap:
³ And he shall sit as a refiner and purifier of silver: and he shall purify the sons of Levi, and purge them as gold and silver, that they may offer unto the Lord an offering in righteousness.⁶ For I am the Lord, I change not; therefore ye sons of Jacob are not consumed.

I Am Calling – Hear My Voice in This Hour

I have heard their cries and have seen all that the oppressor has brought upon them, their children and their relationships. I am sending forth a mighty army of warring saints that are preparing for battle. They are beating their plowing shares and sharpening their sickles that they shall become instruments of the "Gathering."

My harvest is ripened and a time of gleaning is eminent. Prepare your instruments! Bring forth your spears! Put on your armor! The battle has begun and will become more intense as the days go by.

Come into My presence and receive your instructions. Do not fear but trust that I am able to deliver. I have called and I will ensure victory over the enemy. Do not allow the cries and offenses that have kept you in a state of dullness to My voice to prevail any longer.

Listen – I will instruct and encourage your soul. I will save you from the calamities that await the world. You are My voice. Cry aloud – tell My people that I am coming and My reward is with me, says the Lord.

Revelation 14:15 KJV
And another angel came out of the temple, crying with a loud voice to him that sat on the cloud, Thrust in thy sickle, and reap: for the time is come for thee to reap; for the harvest of the earth is ripe.

Joel 3:13 NLT
Swing the sickle, for the harvest is ripe. Come, tread the grapes, for the winepress is full. The storage vats are overflowing with the wickedness of these people."

47

Hidden Treasures

Dear Ones, I have given you abilities that far exceed your human understanding. You have been retrofitted with all of the power necessary to execute the plans that I have made for your life. For whom I foreknew, I also predestined to accomplish the tasks set before them.

Look deeply inside yourself for I have placed hidden treasures within you that will reach beyond your preconceived feelings of inadequacy and provide for you a prescriptive plan for your success. Put into motion the positive ideas and notions that have emerged from the depths of your inner being. You must not be afraid of failure for I have not called you to bring your plan to a place of defeat and failure, but rather to ensure success in that which I have planted in you.

Your feelings of doubt that you can achieve, do not come from Me, My child. A father desires good gifts for his children and will always offer wise counsel and sound advice. I advise you to come out of the circle of doubt and unbelief, because you have continued around this circle far too long. I tell you that this chain will be broken and you will continue along a straight path to success.

Remember Joshua 1:8 – and keep my word ever before you. (Do not let this Book of the Law depart from your mouth; meditate on it day and night, so that you may be careful to do everything written in it. Then you will be prosperous and successful). Also remember that as you meditate on My word, you will receive the power to succeed.

Remove yourself from the company of complainers and backbiters, and from those who are quick to utter discouragement. These cannot see, for they are blind and hurry to sit in the presence of the blind, to receive their direction. You will never prosper in the company of naysayers, Beloved. I have shown you the way. Believe Me. I long, to bless you. The blessing is not only for you, but for generations to come. Through your faithfulness, many will be blessed and find their way home. Put your faith to work for you. I will open doors that no man can shut. Did I not tell you that this is the season of open doors? Do not throw your seed away, but plant it so that it brings forth fruit. Remember that your seed is perpetual My child, and capable of bringing life to dead situations. Do not allow your abilities and plans to shrivel like the barren fig tree.

Colossians 2:2-3 (NIV)
My goal is that they may be encouraged in heart and united in love, so that they may have the full riches of complete understanding, in order that they may know the mystery of God, namely, Christ, 3 in whom are hidden all the treasures of wisdom and knowledge.

No Time to Wait

Now is the time to hurry and be about your Father's business Beloved. There is no time to wait – languishing behind while others who started out with you have long since responded to My call. The five foolish virgins knew that their lamps were to be trimmed at all times, because they had no idea when the Bridegroom would appear. They knew what was required, but failed to prepare because it appeared that they had plenty of time. I tell you that you must hurry My children. There is no time to wait!

Matthew 25:10
But while they were on their way to buy the oil, the bridegroom arrived. The virgins who were ready went in with him to the wedding banquet. And the door was shut.

The Highway of Life

Recently, my husband was diagnosed with cancer and I was taken utterly by surprise. As long as we live on this earth, we must all travel the highway of life and at some point, we will come up against a speed bump, a roadblock, or another impediment. We know that in this life, we will have tribulations, however, that does not quite ring true to us until calamity comes and strikes in a very real and tangible way. It is then that we assess our own mortality, and come to the realization that only God is eternal and immortal. There is an appointed time for all things. However, I have learned during my tenure on earth, that our prayers influence God. I am reminded of how the prophet Jeremiah prayed to God; (Jeremiah 10:23-24 NASB) "I know, O Lord, that a man's way is not in himself, Nor is it in a man who walks to direct his steps." The Prophet Jeremiah prayed to God for healing in this way; "Lord, You are the giver of life. You are the one who has always supplied your people with life and health and strength. You are the one who can even raise one up from his death-bed, so that in the 'Third Day,' he may go into your temple and glorify you. You are the one O Lord, that grants life to your people. You are the one who raises the dead."

One day while visiting my husband in the hospital, he asked if I would read a scripture before I left. I opened the bible and began to read Psalms 91 and these verses (14-16) took my breath away:

Psalms 91:14-16 (KJV)
14 Because he hath set his love upon me, therefore will I deliver him: I will set him on high, because he hath known my name.
15 He shall call upon me, and I will answer him: I will be with him in trouble; I will deliver him, and honor him.
16 With long life will I satisfy him, and shew him my salvation.

Beloved, what you have had to bear, is nothing in comparison to the endless numbers of times that I have called out to My children in an effort to prevent them from stepping out onto the highway of life, totally unprepared and unequipped for the journey. Many continue to encircle the path year after year, suffering the same losses, encountering the same dangers, totally unaware.

I have prepared road maps and set up signs along the way, so that My children may obtain easy access to their destinations, but very few received and followed the directions mapped out within their "trip plans." Many do not even have a trip plan.

Dear one, do not allow your lack of trust to hinder you. Have I not told you that, I will make the crooked places plain and I will even make a way in the desert for you? Trust and do not doubt My child. I have promised never to leave you alone.

The Prescriptive Plan

Dear ones, I have given you abilities that far exceed your human understanding. You have been retrofitted with all the power necessary to execute the plans that I have made for your life. For whom I foreknew, I also predestinated to accomplish the tasks set before you.

Look deeply inside yourself, for I have placed hidden treasures within you that will reach beyond your preconceived feelings of inadequacy and provide for you a prescriptive plan for your success. Put into motion the ideas and notions that have emerged from the depths of your inner being. You must not be afraid of failure for I have not called you to bring your plan to a place of defeat and failure, but rather to ensure success in that that which I have planted in you.

Your feelings of doubt that you can achieve, does not come from Me My Child. A Father desires good gifts for his children and will always offer wise counsel and sound advice. I advise you to come out of the circle of doubt and unbelief because you have continued around this circle far too long. I tell you that this chain will be broken and you will continue along a straight path to success. Remember Joshua 1:8 and keep My word ever before you. Also remember that as you meditate on My word, you will have the power to succeed.

Remove yourself from the company of complainers and backbiters and from those who are quick to utter discouragement. These cannot see for they are blind and hurry to sit in the presence of the blind to receive their direction. You will never prosper in the company of naysayers beloved. I have shown you the way. Believe Me. I long to bless you.

The blessing is not only for you but for generations to come. Through your faithfulness many will be blessed and find their way home. Put your faith to work for you. I will open doors that no man can shut. Did I not tell you that this is the season of open doors? Do not throw your seed away but plant it so that it brings forth fruit. Remember that your seed is perpetual My child and capable of bringing life to dead situations. Do not allow your abilities and plans to shrivel like the fig tree.

Revelation 4:1 (KJV)
After this I looked, and, behold, a door was opened in heaven: and the first voice which I heard was as it were of a trumpet talking with me; which said, Come up hither, and I will shew thee things which must be hereafter.

Disappointments

Do not be dismayed when others hurt and disappoint you. These minor afflictions are just what you need to assist with your growth. Disappointments are only temporary stumbling blocks which are often used as speed bumps along the highway of life. These bumps are used as instruments to remind you that you must slow down, so that your travel along the highway of life does not become to you a racetrack of hurt, defeat, heartache and impending life-threatening danger. You must be reminded that you can do nothing without Me.

Too often My people do not seek the My Wisdom as they chart the course of this highway. To proceed on this highway without a roadmap is a very dangerous endeavor and one which could cost very dearly.

My children, I stand ready to remove the speed bumps from your path, so that you may proceed on your journey with success in view. You must note that I have created you in My image and therefore you are also filled with creative abilities which are waiting to be released. But the releasing of these great and marvelous gifts comes by degree. When you move too quickly in your own will, you stand to veer off the straight and narrow highway and in so doing you head directly for spiritual and often physical destruction.

It is then that I place the greatest speed bumps in your path. I will never lose anyone that My Father has given Me. The problem with My children is that they become blinded with the lust of the eyes, the lust of the flesh and the pride of life, which causes them to desire the pleasures of sin for a season and miss the opportunity of acquiring life eternal with Me. Dear Ones, these choices bring disappointment to both you and me. You must remember that the reason I died, was so that you would escape the disappointment of hell for eternity. Each incident of disappointment brings forth growth.

Joshua 1:9 (NASB)
"Have I not commanded you? Be strong and courageous! Do not tremble or be dismayed, for the LORD your God is with you wherever you go."

1 Peter 5:10-11 (KJV)
10 But the God of all grace, who hath called us unto his eternal glory by Christ Jesus, after that ye have suffered a while, make you perfect, stablish, strengthen, settle you.
11 To him be glory and dominion for ever and ever. Amen.

In Everything Give Thanks

Dear Ones, "in the world you shall have tribulations but be of good cheer for I have overcome the world." Many are experiencing very difficult times. Your trials are greater than in past times, but I have already told you that you would have "fewer, but greater" trials this year. You are an Overcomer!

Many of you are looking for the "New Beginnings" promised earlier in the year. I tell you that the time has come. It is upon you now. Your trials have become "stepping stones" which have lifted you to new levels of devotion and obedience. Your "change" has begun to take form even in a time that you are unable to recognize what is happening in your spiritual life. This change will surely come about in the natural realm as you begin to "Give Thanks" for restoration and renewal. Give Thanks my beloved, even in the midst of your trials, for this will become your stepping stone to greater success in My Kingdom.

1 Thessalonians 5:18 (KJV)
In every thing give thanks: for this is the will of God in Christ Jesus concerning you.

The Fragments

Beloved, you have poured out from the anointing that has been given to you and at times you feel that you have completely exhausted the supply. Never concern yourself with how I choose to use you, because there is an unending supply of My Grace and My Love stored up within you. Do you not remember how I fed the 5000 with 2 small fish and 5 loaves? Do you not remember that even after all had eaten and were full there were fragments remaining, enough to fill 12 baskets? I tell you that I am the same God; your Jehovah Jireh who always supplies more than enough.

Go forth, and continue to pour out upon My people that which I have supplied for their needs. Many will be saved, set free, and delivered. Yes, I am the "God of the Miraculous" and I am fully prepared to send you forth in this hour, for you have desired more of Me. You have desired the double portion anointing and you will see it manifested in this hour. Yes, the fragments of this anointing will bless thousands.

I know that you are unable to see this in the natural, but look deeply into the spirit realm and I will show you the many souls that will be saved, says the Lord. Do not depend upon your intellect My children. This work defies your human reasoning. Surely there are places where thousands gather, but they gather to hear the swelling deceitful words that come from the intellect of man. These words give false hope to many who have itching ears and are blinded by the lust of the eyes, the lust of the flesh, and the pride of life. Even the fragments that I have placed within you will do more to satisfy the hungry soul.

Luke 9:16-17 (KJV)
16Then he took the five loaves and the two fishes, and looking up to heaven, he blessed them, and brake, and gave to the disciples to set before the multitude. *17And they did eat, and were all*

filled: and there was taken up of fragments that remained to them twelve baskets.

Obedience

Beloved, when your heart is open to obey My Word; and your ear is open to hear the voice of My Spirit, I am free to fill your life with the abundance of My grace. Have I not told you that Obedience is better than sacrifice?

I stand ready to bless My children and supply you with daily benefits which have been stored up for you; awaiting your submission to My will, so that you may experience a mighty "release" of My glory in your life. There is no gift or sacrifice that will substitute for your simply yielding your heart to My will. There is no need for you to suffer lack. I stand ready and waiting to pour out your portion in this hour. Do not harden your heart to instruction and the voice of My anointed servants, who have been chosen to bring you "good news" and tidings of great joy.

You are looking for My blessings to come from directions in which I have not sent them, and from voices which I have not raised up in this hour. Listen to the voices of those whom I have chosen to deliver My word, which I have sent to you. There are many fathers and mothers Beloved, but not many teachers. Receive the glad tidings and instructions that I am sending to you and you will experience "restoration and abundance." Give Thanks and remain in a ready state of "obedience" to My will for your life. For this is My will concerning you, says the Lord.

1 Samuel 15:22 (NIV)
But Samuel replied: "Does the LORD delight in burnt offerings and sacrifices as much as in obeying the voice of the LORD? To obey is better than sacrifice, and to heed (listen) is better than the fat of rams.

Haggai 1:12 (NIV)Then Zerubbabel son of Shealtiel, Joshua son of Jehozadak, the high priest, and the whole remnant of the people obeyed the voice of the LORD their God and the message of the prophet Haggai, because the LORD their God had sent him. And the people feared the LORD.

The Heavenly Trading Floor - A Time of Release and Exchange
Beloved, it is time for my people to know and understand that this is a time of "Release and Exchange." I will use this moment to teach you the significance of the *"Heavenly Trading Floor."* For it is at the *Trading Floor*, that you will leave your broken dreams and broken lives. In exchange, I will give you hope and a future. It is where you will trade your sickness and disease for wholeness, health and healing. I will trade with you, new parts for those that are in need of replacement.

This is a place of elevation and promotion. I will even *"Blow the Breath of My Spirit"* upon those seeds that have been previously planted within you and you shall ascend from the bottom to the top; from death to life; from obscurity to recognition, from the floor to the ceiling. This is a time of "Releasing, Perfecting and Restoring."

Many have received the mighty power-gifts of the Apostolic and the Prophetic anointing during this trading floor experience. There shall be a great *Outpouring* in this season. Let the river flow. Let the rains fall. Walk in the *Overflow* anointing. Let the seed bring forth; let it bud, burst and bring forth fruit; this is the season. Activate your faith and ascend. This is the season; the season to *"Release and Bring Forth."* Bring your lack and need to the *Trading Floor* and I will exchange it for abundance and excess.

2 Corinthians 8:9 (NIV)
For you know the grace of our Lord Jesus Christ, that though he was rich, yet for your sake he became poor, so that you through his poverty might become rich.

Lazarus Come Forth

Too long you have been bound with the grave clothes of defeat. I am sending a power that will release you and set you free. It is time for you to arise from the grave of oppression, depression, suppression, fear and intimidation. Take flight upon Eagle's wings My Beloved, and soar above your present circumstances. Leave behind all that has held you back and weighted you down. I am bringing life into your broken spirit. This life shall come from the depths of your inner being as My Spirit communes and calls forth that which has been stored up within you. My Spirit is restoring your soul that your soul may live. Rise up and take on new life. I am calling you – "Come forth."

John 11:44 (NIV)
The dead man came out, his hands and feet wrapped with strips of linen, and a cloth around his face. Jesus said to them, "Take off the grave clothes and let him go."

Bring It to Me

Did you know that you can cast all of your cares on Me because I care so much for you? You do not need to bear the stress of these burdens alone. I am releasing thousands of angels to engage in serious warfare for your soul. There is a war going on in the heavenlies; a battle in which you will not need to fight. This battle requires that you to simply engage yourself in prayer and totally release all of your cares into my hands.

The enemy desires to confuse you and cause you to engage in this battle, but you have only to rejoice in Me because the battle has already been won. Satan has been defeated and subdued. Trust that I am fully able to overcome your enemies (seen and unseen), and cause them to retreat and flee from the intensity and heat of this battle. I have positioned and engaged the mighty bludgeoning forces of My "Battering Ram" and have totally crushed your enemies.

I have sent my Word and healed you and delivered you out of every stressful and dangerous situation. It is time My child, for you to truly come to the realization that I am your shield and buckler. Make no mistake about it; the battle is intense, your soul has been targeted and Satan has fired the weapons of defeat, stress, distress, despair and helplessness against you. I will protect you from every missile and fiery dart that Satan hurls at you. You will indeed overcome these attacks as you purpose yourself to "put on the garment of praise for the spirit of heaviness."

I will even cause you to sing a new song in the very midst of this battle; one which even the angels cannot sing. For it shall be a song of deliverance and a mantra that brings forth new life, meaning, and purpose, says the Lord. You have only to bring it to Me. For I have already put upon you the "full armor of God" in the spirit realm and you have only to stand!

64

2 Chronicles 20:17 (KJV)
"Ye shall not need to fight in this battle: set yourselves, stand ye still, and see the salvation of the LORD with you, O Judah and Jerusalem: fear not, nor be dismayed; tomorrow go out against them: for the LORD will be with you."

Isaiah 42:10 (NASB)
Sing to the LORD a new song, His praise from the ends of the earth, you who go down to the sea, and all that is in it, you islands, and all who live in them.

A Time of Decision

I am calling my people into a time of decision. It is time to decide whose side you will choose. The time for indecision is over. You must realize that your continued existence is dependent upon the choices that you make in this hour. Remember that a wavering man is like a wave tossed and driven by every wind of doctrine and that man is unstable in all his ways; in relationships, in business, and most assuredly in the things of the Kingdom.

It is time that you emerge from the valley of indecision and rise up to the mountain heights of commitment, consignment, continuity, transformation, and completeness of the Kingdom of God. You have only to surrender your will to mine and seek My face. Your destiny is waiting for you to assume your position and gain momentum through prayer and meditating on My Word.

As you surrender to My calling, you will emerge from the deep abyss of indecision and begin to operate in your predestinated "function"." Your surroundings and exterior façade will begin to fade as you gain new status, control and Kingdom Advance. Your past confusion will fade in the light of your new found life and wisdom.

You have wasted so much time. You have missed so many opportunities. I tell you that time awaits no one. The hour is late. Take your position and begin to operate in your calling; your "function" while today is yet today. You have only to make that decision. My Servant Joshua did; "As for me and my house, we shall serve the Lord." The choice is yours.

Joshua 24:14-15 (NKJV)
14 "Now therefore fear the Lord and serve him in sincerity and in faithfulness. Put away the gods that your fathers served beyond the River and in Egypt, and serve the Lord. 15 And if it is

evil in your eyes to serve the Lord, choose this day whom you will serve, whether the gods your fathers served in the region beyond the River, or the gods of the Amorites in whose land you dwell. But as for me and my house, we will serve the Lord."

Doris M. Richardson

I Have Not Left You

I have not left you. This is the time of testing that was spoken of before. Do you still say "yes" to My will? This time of proving will bring about an incomparable strength My Beloved. You will emerge from this testing period with a resiliency that will cause you to spring back, recoil, and resume your shape no matter how hard the bending process may be. Often My children will cry out for Me to lighten the load and lessen the pressure. However, you must go through this process of proving in order to move to the next level of My Glory.

Remember, I am with you always, and will bear your burden when the load becomes too much for you to bear. You must go through this phase in order to really appreciate the blessings that I have set apart for you. Yes there is a time of great reaping and great reward stored up for you. You have sensed My presence in times of peace and stillness and now you must search for the refreshing notes after the storm and the rain.

Yes, there is a refreshing awaiting you, and you will begin to appreciate the rewards of a fresh anointing of My Spirit of Grace and Mercy in these times. I am beginning to pour out My mercy and grace upon you and I will settle your spirit, says the Lord.

My peace I leave with you My Beloved, as you make your way to the place that has been reserved just for you. Come – Come – Come. I will give you rest. Cease from your struggles. I will begin to show you how I will cause your enemies to cease from their attacks against you. I have seen your struggles. I have heard your cries. I have answered – yea and amen.

Cease from your struggles and watch me work. I am a burden bearer, a strong tower; a great deliverer; a way maker; an open door; the Prince of Peace; more than enough; a ram in the bush;

a light in the darkness; rest for the weary; bread for the hungry; water for the thirsty; shelter from the storm.

Psalms 18:10 (KJV)
The name of the Lord is a strong tower: the righteous runneth into it, and is safe.

Refocus

Take this time to refocus your eyes in the direction of the Spirit, where there is sight. You have not seen the things that are coming in the days ahead because your attention has been on things gone by. Yesterday is gone and sufficient for the day are the things that are fleeting by, before your very eyes so quickly, that if you blink they are gone and if they are gone, they are forgotten instantly. There is so much to steal your attention and your minds. You must stop now, and make a conscious effort to refocus.

Matthew 6:34 (KJV)
Take therefore no thought for the morrow: for the morrow shall take thought for the things of itself. Sufficient unto the day is the evil thereof.

The Depth of Your Praise

I am bringing forth a praise that will arise from your deepest parts. A praise that will resonate and pierce the ears of the enemy, a praise of victory! I have brought you through the darkest, most dismal times of your life into a time of light and rejoicing! This praise will spring forth and penetrate the place of your despair, loneliness and intimidation. You will soar to higher heights as you leave the place of your former desolation. This will be an expression of the joy that will come forth following a time of weeping which endured through your night, or time of intense darkness. The morning light has come and the Son of Righteousness has broken through to spawn the Dawning of a New Day, a new life with Me in the Light of My presence. This great light which is the reflection of my Holiness, has come upon you My child and you shall dwell in my perpetual "Secret Place," says the Lord.

Psalm 30:5 (KJV)
"Weeping may endure for a night, but joy cometh in the morning."

1 Peter 2:9 (NIV)
"But you are a chosen people, a royal priesthood, a holy nation, a people belonging to God, that you may declare the praises of him who called you out of darkness into his wonderful light."

A Time of "Ascension" In the Kingdom

Beloved, you are about to soar to heights unknown and I will cause your elevation and your flight to be seamless (flawless) and secure (safe/protected). The levels that you are about to ascend to will transcend (go beyond) all human knowledge. New levels of understanding, hope, and security are about to unfold in your midst and these levels will be your spring-board (launching pad) as you continue to rise and soar in My kingdom.

The heights that you are ascending to, requires you to be completely focused on the things which are above, and to be willing to leave your present position behind. New relationships in the spirit will emerge and these will require much prayer on your part. You will not be able to go where I am taking you until you know complete surrender. This new position requires a humility and willingness to forsake all that you presently know to be safe and secure.

There is no security in your stuff or your present financial state. You must be willing to leave it all behind as this journey will be one in which, absolutely no excess baggage will be tolerated. I tell you that you must forsake all, for this ascension will take place so quickly that there will not be time enough to collect your stuff. I am calling you to an area of heightened awareness in My Spirit in these days so that you may be sustained.

Remember that I am your "Keeper." Stay close to Me. Bring all that is dear to you, near to Me. Pray for your present condition that you may not be hindered by it. Nothing is as important as spending time in My presence. Remember that the gold and the silver is mine and I will disperse them as it pleases Me.

This is a time of "Acquisition." I am pouring My blessings upon My people and they will acquire wealth, wisdom, insight, and ability to rightfully disburse these blessings in the Kingdom.

Transition, acquisition, and disbursement will begin to flow in My Kingdom in these days says the Lord.

Colossians 3:2-3 (NKJV)
2 Set your mind on things above, not on things on the earth. 3 For you died, and your life is hidden with Christ in God. 4 When Christ who is our life appears, then you also will appear with Him in glory.

Draw Closer To Me

Draw closer to Me, My people. I am calling you to a place of refuge from the storm; a place of safety from the battles that have confronted and will confront you. In this place you will find comfort under My covering. In this place you will learn of Me. You will be taught by My Spirit, the strategies necessary for your survival from impending wars; perils and calamities which are soon to be released upon the earth realm.

This time of drawing will bring forth a deeper desire to know Me. You have only to quiet yourself in order to hear My call; to sense My drawing. You must eliminate all unnecessary clamor and senseless distractions. Increase your time of personal worship as it is in the worship that you will find a greater release of My Glory. My Glory will be a shield over you, which will begin to diffuse through your mind in such a miraculous way, that you will immediately perceive and discern all spirits in your midst.

Your vision will become keen so that you will be able to see beyond the natural into the spirit realm – yes, you will have many open visions. But this vision that will come upon you as a result of the release of My Glory upon you, will cause you to see that which is immediately around you thus giving you the opportunity to make swift decisions. The effects of this Glory will cause a deeper understanding of My word. For it is given unto you to know the mysteries (hidden things), of the Kingdom of God.

As you draw closer, you will be strengthened spiritually and enabled to "execute," says the Lord. Come.

James 4:8 (NKJV)
Draw near to God and He will draw near to you. Cleanse your hands, you sinners; and purify your hearts, you double-minded.

James 4:7-10 (The Message)
So let God work his will in you. Yell a loud no to the Devil and watch him scamper. Say a quiet yes to God and he'll be there in no time. Quit dabbling in sin. Purify your inner life. Quit playing the field. Hit bottom, and cry your eyes out. The fun and games are over. Get serious, really serious. Get down on your knees before the Master; it's the only way you'll get on your feet.

When Things Go Wrong

Beloved, when things seem to go wrong with your plans and the course of your life seems to take a swift turn; do not always be so quick to attribute this to Satan and the sprits of darkness. As I have told you in the past and yet again I speak to you, not in dark passages that cannot be understood, but plainly so that you will clearly perceive that My thoughts are not your thoughts, neither are My ways, your ways.

Often the very plans which you have so carefully executed, are not My plans for your life. For I know the plans that I have for you. I alone, have plotted out the course of your Destiny. Because you have a tendency to take your eyes off the course, you are bound by time and space in this present world. Circumstances and situations surrounding your life will often tempt you to divert and abort your purpose.

My love for you which knows no boundaries, will cause Me to place a stumbling block before you in order to bring you to full dependency on me. It is during these times that you cry out to Me for deliverance but I will not remove My hand until you clearly surrender to My will. I do not delight in seeing your sufferings; but these momentary afflictions are often self-imposed by your abstinence, disobedience, and lack of faith.

Wait on Me beloved and be of good courage; for indeed I will give you the strength to endure and be victorious. I will teach you to weigh the matter and you will be quick to resume the course of your Destiny and walk in faith and obedience to My will for your life. When things seem to go wrong, I am busy rearranging the course of your Destiny.

When the time is complete I will remove the stumbling blocks. I will keep your heart and your mind during these times. Trust Me, says the Lord. Trust Me with your life.

Romans 8:28 (KJV)
"And we know that all things work together for good to them that love God, to them who are the called according to his purpose."

See

I know that it has been a while since you have heard from me however, your footprints are etched upon my heart and I have not forgotten you. Often one must spend time meditating and hearing from the Lord for the situations that are affecting those whom we love so dearly. Remember that my love for you is merely a weakened version of His love that flows through me. Weakened by the limitations of my flesh which could never love you so completely. Is not our Father "awesome?" What manner of love is this? Surely I could never go the distance and bear it out so gloriously. However, within the capacity that lies within me to love all of you ....I do. Hear the word of the Lord:

Lift up your head to see the good that I am doing to bring you out of established patterns, for you cannot progress until these corrections are made. You must see in the realm of the Spirit to begin to understand the value of the tests and trials that you are now enduring. As long as you can only see with your physical eyes instead of your spiritual eyes, you will become a victim of your circumstances and will only grumble and complain as you dump down into self-pity. I tell you the truth. This attitude is not only of the flesh and carnal, but it is also demonic in nature. But you, beloved, belong to Me. It would be in your best interest to rise up and rejoice in this important work, says the Lord.

2 Corinthians 7:1 (KJV)
Therefore, having these promises, beloved, let us cleanse ourselves from all filthiness of the flesh and spirit, perfecting holiness in the fear of God.

This is not the time to crumble under the pressure of your responsibilities. Rather, rise up in faith. Trust Me to enable you to go beyond your physical and emotional limitations, to complete the tasks at hand. I will give you extraordinary strength to meet every challenge. Ask Me to stretch your time and I will do so, says the Lord. I will make a way where there seems to be no way. Rise up and go forth in victory.

2 Corinthians 12:9 (KJV)
And he said unto me, My grace is sufficient for thee: for my strength is made perfect in weakness. Most gladly therefore will I rather glory in my infirmities, that the power of Christ may rest upon me.

Section 3

Welcome to the Mountain

Your Grace

Lord, from my heart I cry out to You. My soul declares that there is no one like You. For who would rush to bless one so undeserved? To make a way when all resources have dried up? To pour out unconditional love and tender mercies in the darkest hour? The answer is found in only you; for You alone are the *Answer*. Your grace is poured out upon me in the dayspring unsparingly, in great measure. Lord, where would I be without Your grace?

Lord, it is when I am at my lowest that You come and pick me up from the valley of pain and despair. Like King David, surely "it was good that I was afflicted." For it is often in my affliction that my heart begins to understand the depths of Your love and Your grace.

It is Your grace; yes Your lovingkindness that is apportioned to me and keeps me each day. There is absolutely nothing that I can do, or have done in the past to deserve Your favor and your amazing grace upon my life. Truly, You are an awesome wonder, a Mighty God of Mercy and Grace. Your grace will undo the harm that the enemy has caused. Your Grace breaks the chains of heaviness, removes the yokes of bondage and causes me to live a victorious life!

Jeremiah 10:6 (NIV)
LORD, there is no one like you! For you are great, and your name is full of power.

Quiet Your Spirit

Beloved, do not fear, fret or doubt. My promises are true and you are safe and secure in My word. The shield of My love covers you at all times, even when you think I am not near.

You must learn to quiet your human spirit even when the storms are brewing, so that you may able to discern the direction, severity and intended impact of the storm. In so doing, you will (without fear or foreboding), redirect the storm and diminish its intensity and impact.

Remember that My love enfolds, covers and keeps you safe. As you quiet your spirit and meditate upon My word, you will become keenly aware of My inexhaustible daily supply of mercy. You may rest assured that My lovingkindness is even better than life itself. Be still beloved. Be still, let go and surrender.

Psalm 46:10 (NIV)
He says, "Be still, and know that I am God; I will be exalted among the nations, I will be exalted in the earth."

Do Not Concentrate on Your Present Circumstance

Beloved, the pendulum is about to swing in the opposite direction and the flow of your current circumstance will reverse. You are expending entirely too much energy on the issues that you currently face, or least, that which seems so real to your senses. Yes, you may be currently in the realm of discomfort and your soul may be disquieted (worried/anxious) within you, for lack of identification of an immediate fix or solution. But I am bringing you into an entirely different level of being, where the reality shall be totally opposite of all that you have believed true, in the (not so distant) past. You will awaken to a new concept of sight and vision, which you would have thought totally foreign until now.

Your eyes will begin to capture glimpses of light in this strata and will immediately interpret them as illuminous strokes of lightening, on a canvas beautifully glowing with the wondrous fiery storms emitted as the light passes over fields of diamonds, glowing in the morning sun. Before this time, your mind would not even allow you to see and comprehend such a sight, but somehow in this place, (even as awesome as it may be) it seems all too familiar and ordinary. As you raise your head to take in more of this great fiery display, suddenly, you are immersed into a great chasm of absolute stillness and visual awe. Sight in this place has become heightened to the point of a brilliance which has never been seen before. Your eyes have surely been lifted into a realm of glorious beauty not inhibited by the mechanics of human sight. Stand and be amazed as I cause you to see beyond your natural ability, into the very realms of heaven.

I am bringing you into a place reserved for those who desire to move forward in the direction of the Spirit; where the picture displayed on the great canvas of life is completely opposite to that which you are being shown in the earthly realms of your current circumstance. What I am showing you beloved, is the answer to the petitions that you have placed before me. Rejoice! The situation that you are currently experiencing no longer exists, for I have moved forward into your future to cause a "turnaround" in your circumstance. The shifting took place the moment that you called and I answered. Now, open your eyes and see that I have turned that thing around for you.

1 Corinthians 2:9 (NKJV)
But as it is written:
"Eye has not seen, nor ear heard, Nor have entered into the heart of man The things which God has prepared for those who love Him."

Have You Lowered Your Guard?

Beloved, do not let your guard down. You cannot afford to allow anything to penetrate your armor. You must guard your heart with all diligence, for out of it comes the issues of life. Satan seeks to bring you false illusions of despair and heavy heartedness. But I tell you to put on the garments of praise at this hour and offer up your sacrifices of praise and I will receive your praise and send down the blessings that you need so much. Why is your soul cast down? Why does the spirit of depression and despair follow you? Put your trust in Me and I will replace your despair with hope. For I alone am your "Blessed Hope."

I am searching for those in this hour who have come to the end of themselves. Those who are tired of leaning on the arms of flesh to bring them love, joy, and peace. I desire to bless you and to load you with benefits every day. Why do you think that I am a sometime God? Come to Me and I will equip you daily with all that you need for the battle. I will even fight for you.

Proverbs 4:23-27 (The Message)
Keep vigilant watch over your heart; that's where life starts. Don't talk out of both sides of your mouth; avoid careless banter, white lies, and gossip. Keep your eyes straight ahead; ignore all sideshow distractions. Watch your step, and the road will stretch out smooth before you. Look neither right nor left; leave evil in the dust.

Doris M. Richardson

You Must Not Tire Now

Beloved, in your weariness the enemy has tried to convince you that you are too tired continue on. You must not listen to the lies of Satan. Have I not told you? Have you not heard that I will give strength to the weak? You have persevered through the most difficult times. Are they not behind you?

Do not give up-do not give in. Your prophesy is working for you a great recompense of reward. I have seen your sufferings. I have heard your cries. I am here to deliver you from all of them. Aspire to keep your thoughts pure by meditating on Me; on My word. I will bring peace and soundness of mind, body, and soul.

A little suffering is necessary to build your faith and elevate you, to the degree that I need you to be able to function in, for My Glory. I am beginning to pour out My Spirit in such a measure that has never been manifested before, because the troubles of the world are about to reach an all-time high. Many will lose their balance and go reeling because their feet are not firmly planted on solid ground.

This is the time to make wise decisions and continue to stand. Do not go running after that which satisfies temporarily, nor should you be enticed by those who seem to have access to money. If you just trust Me, I will show you how to survive these times and obtain all that you need. Do not take your eyes off Me nor trust in the system; for the system is designed to hold you in bondage. You are not a slave! Don't faint now.

Isaiah 40:28-31 (NIV)
Do you not know? Have you not heard? The LORD is the everlasting God, the Creator of the ends of the earth. He will not grow tired or weary, and his understanding no one can fathom. He gives strength to the weary and increases the power of the weak. Even youths grow tired and weary, and

young men stumble and fall; but those who hope in the LORD will renew their strength. They will soar on wings like eagles; they will run and not grow weary, they will walk and not be faint.

Requisition

Go ahead – prepare the requisition for I am about to release the Latter Rain upon My people who have panted for me like the deer by the water brook. You have only to ask in order to acquire this end time release of my anointing. Until now, many have sought merely to acquire treasures on earth. But My army which I am preparing in this hour, have sought primarily to please Me. They have longed to be equipped for battle; they have sought to be filled with My Spirit; to acquire spiritual gifts for the edification of My Body.

They have not sought after earthly riches and the wealth of kings. They have asked for Godly wisdom as did My servant Solomon. They have sought Godly integrity as did My servant Joseph, and Godly discretion as did my servant Daniel. Therefore, unto these I will fulfill their requisition in this hour, for they have acquired the Former Rain anointing of those who have gone before and to that, I will pour out the double portion blessing of the latter rain anointing for this current hour of acquisition, says the Lord.

This acquisition shall be disbursed among My people; My army. This great acquisition shall be all that is necessary for My mighty army to go forth and be a blessing to my people. The spirit of giving shall be awakened and many shall come out of years of poverty and lack. There will be no false requirements attached to the blessings that I shall pour out in this hour.

I tell you that My requirements have not changed. They are written in the scriptures and are plain. Prepare the requisition.

Joshua 1:8 (KJV)
"And this book of the law shall not depart out of thy mouth; but thou shall meditate therein day and night; that thou mayest observe to do all that is written therein; for then thou shall

make thy way prosperous, and then thou shall have good success.

Don't Give Up

Don't give up; you're almost there. To stop short of your goal is to not see My goodness. The truth is that NO weapon formed against you shall prosper and every tongue that rises up against you in judgment is condemned. I tell you that breakthrough is absolutely imminent. Refuse to waver in your hope, but rather hold fast the beginning of your hope steadfast until the end. I have made a way through this winding path that leads ever upward to your destiny. Follow My leading, says the Lord.

Hebrews 10:23 (KJV)
Let us hold fast the confession of our hope without wavering, for He who promised is faithful.

The Power to Restore

Know that I have called you and designed it to be so. I have equipped you with the necessary giftings and anointing to carry out My plan and My calling upon your life. I will use you in a unique and unusual manner. You will stand before judges and magistrates and pronounce My word and declare my judgments. Many will receive hope, many healings will take place. The dead will live again. Mountains will be removed. Death and hell will not know their place.

The earth will quake, great winds will blow, but my people will survive these storms. I have given my servants the ability to calm these winds and to speak to the mountains, that they may know their place and return thereunto. The earth shall stand still and every rock and stone return to its place when my servants speak and command it to be so. Great power will be demonstrated through my servants, and the world will know that it is I who give them power to RESTORE!

Revelation 1:18 (NIV)
I am the Living One. I was dead, and behold, now I am alive forever and ever! And I hold the keys of Death and of Hades.

Step Near To Me

As you walk in the path that I have chosen, you will find that your feet are firmly planted and moving toward an upward path which leads to eternal life. Obedience to My will is essential as you progress along this way. You will find that the path is narrow, however you must watch and pray continuously as the adversary seeks to cause your feet to stumble.

I will be your guide as you continue to the place that I have prepared for you. But you must purpose yourself not to stop progressing at any point along the way. Never stop unless I stop. In fact, My footsteps will be imprinted along this path and you will find them if you will see with your eyes and believe with all of your heart. It will seem lonely at times along this path, but that is when you must look deeply within your heart for the hidden word.

Remember that I told you "I will never leave you nor forsake you?" You are never alone, even when the pain of the weight that you are bearing seems to be much, too much for you. Why don't you just let go of it? Remember I will take it. I will carry it. Release it to Me.....that son; that daughter; that husband; that wife; your bills; your marriage; your engagement; your job; your position in the church; your friendships; release it all to Me.

I will discard that which did not belong to you in the first place. I will restore the scarred replica which has been broken, shattered, and burned by flaming tongues. Give it to Me and I will fix it. I will make it new. You will be relieved as your walk suddenly progresses to a flight. I will cause you to rise up on Eagle's wings and soar into your destiny, says the Lord.

James 4:8 (NIV)
Come near to God and he will come near to you. Wash your hands, you sinners, and purify your hearts, you double-minded.

Do Not Be Afraid to Step Out

This is the time that I am bringing you into that you will serve me with all of your heart, mind, body and spirit. I am seeking those who would be unreservedly sold out to Me and Me alone. These are very crucial times and require those who would look beyond the comforts of life and lay down their lives for the gospel under any and all conditions. The task is difficult, the reward is great. Seek My voice.... I will tell you what is to come.

I will show you the path that you must take to accomplish my will. My Plan will unfold before you. I will make known to you the strategies that will be used to bring My people out of generations of bondage and deceit. They will be free to worship and serve Me in the true Spirit of Worship. I will restore Holiness to Zion. I will restore peace and I will heal hurts, wounds, diseases, feelings, minds, and relationships. I will also break down and destroy some things. I will remove the detestable things from among you.

I will bring sons and daughters to a place where they will come to reverence the Christ in you more. They will begin to see you as priests in your households and respect the anointing on your lives. I will also bring this move upon your husbands and wives, who have stood idly by as they have watched Me bring you into new levels of My glory. Yes, they have seen this. They have witnessed the change in you. Some have even been secretly jealous and desirous of the qualities that they have seen in this new person that you have become.

For those that have respected My move and My change and have secretly desired it; you will begin to see a change and a sudden shift from where they once were, to actually observing them assume a new position and a new posture in the Ministry. Step aside and allow them to take, (yes take) the position that I have called them to. You will begin to witness a mighty explosion in your ministry. I will send those who will be needy at first, but will also rise up to be a great help to the ministry both financial and spiritually.

Your sons and daughters who have gone astray, following after strange gods, being deceived by doctrines of devils and demon spirits....they shall return. They shall be delivered. Many have been gone for such a very long time. Receive them. I will give you a special grace to minister to them. They will recognize the higher calling on your life and they shall receive Me and be saved.

Fast, pray and search for Me. I am not a God who is far off. I am near. I am always with you. Believe in Me. I will instruct you on how you must lead and nurture My people. I will show you every step that you must take and the path that you must cross. I am with you. I will provide. Do not be afraid to step out. You are fully equipped for the journey; for what lies ahead. Blaze the path.

Acts 2:17-18 (KJV)
17 And it shall come to pass in the last days, saith God, I will pour out of my Spirit upon all flesh: and your sons and your daughters shall prophesy, and your young men shall see visions, and your old men shall dream dreams:

18 And on my servants and on my handmaidens I will pour out in those days of my Spirit; and they shall prophesy:

Seek Me

Seek Me. Search for me for I have great truths to share with you. Know that it is I. I have lifted you from the shadows, I will bring you forth from the place of obscurity into a place of great light and focus. And that light shall be my Spirit over you. Trust in me especially in these time when it seems that things are not progressing quickly enough. Trust me for I have ordained it to be so. I will not force you.

You must be willing and obedient to my calling and my pressing. Remain in the flow of my Spirit. My anointing is upon you to perform a mighty work in these end-times. I have not forgotten you. You have asked, Lord when? When will you send me? When will I go? When shall it be my time? I tell you that the time has come upon you. Now is that time. You must go now. You must move swiftly. I have anointed you to go forth.

Stay connected to my life line. Times are truly difficult. Many are looking to the wrong sources. I will send those who are in need; those who are sinking; those whose hearts are failing because they have set their affections on mere man. They have lost sight. They have blind hope. They will come and be connected.

Pray......Pray for the world's situation; pray for the nations; pray for the church, pray for the leaders that give my people false hope. I am their blessed hope. I am their only hope. They must turn their affection to me. Notice how I have spoken.....This time it is pleading. It shall not always be a pleading voice that you will hear. I will also speak judgment and my judgment will be without mercy, without repentance. So long have I waited for my people to love me, to obey me. I am waiting still. Tell them how much I love them, how much I long for their affection. Tell them that I am waiting still.

2 Peter 3:9 (KJV)
The Lord is not slack concerning his promise, as some men count slackness; but is longsuffering to us-ward, not willing that any should perish, but that all should come to repentance.

Precious Blood

Remove the scales from your eyes. Seek me and live. I do not delight in your offerings - your praise has become putrid to me. I will not allow you to continue to trample My blood underfoot. It is too precious. You do not understand what the blood of My Son has accomplished for you. What it has purchased for you. It is of great price; yes, it is precious. Nothing has greater value! Nothing has accomplished as much!

Do you not know that were it not for My mercies thou would have been totally consumed? Yet you say unto Me, "You are faithful." You utter it with your mouth, but your heart is far from me. Seek me and live! I have given you the greatest gift that will ever be offered unto you. Yet in return, you trample it under foot. I am not pleased with your doings.

But I will pardon you if ye seek me with you whole heart. Keep nothing back for yourselves. Give all - just as I have done. Give all; your whole heart. I will cleanse it; I will make it new; I will restore; I will replenish; I will build up; I will establish.

Hebrews 10:29 (NIV)
How much more severely do you think someone deserves to be punished who has trampled the Son of God underfoot, who has treated as an unholy thing the blood of the covenant that sanctified them, and who has insulted the Spirit of grace?

97

A Time of Darkness in America's Economy

There is a level of my Glory that you have not seen. I will reveal my Glory unto you. I will take you to a higher level of my Glory. There is coming a time of darkness on the earth realm like there never been before. Men's hearts have become cold. Great nations will fall. America's economy will plummet; thus throwing her into great fear and trepidation. Men of great wealth shall tremble and quake for there shall be no safety in their riches.

But the poor shall dwell in safety. The church shall emerge as a great haven for peace and tranquility. I shall show my people how to survive these times. I shall prepare them even now for what lies ahead.

There shall be confusion among the wise and prudent men of the earth; but they shall seek the wisdom of my prophets. This shall be a global move. Nations shall fall even in the east and the west and this hazardous landslide of occurrences shall not subside until I have accomplished my plan. Then shall I return to gather my people unto myself. I shall be their God and they shall be my people forever. There shall be many events that will take place as a precursor to this sure disaster. Yes, they are even taking form now. These things shall be fulfilled in a very short time.

Warn the Nations! Warn my people! Tell them to prepare for there shall surely be perilous times upon the face of the earth! Tell them to return unto their God. For I will surely heal them. For I am a loving and forgiving God! I am gathering my people unto myself. I will protect them from this calamity.

Isaiah 60:1-2
¹Arise shine for thy light is come, and the glory of the Lord is risen upon thee. ²For, behold, the darkness shall cover the earth,

and gross darkness the people; but the glory of the Lord shall arise upon thee, and his glory shall be seen upon thee.

A Forgiving Father

For thou hast wept sore before me for my people; in this I am well pleased. Take courage in this; I the Lord have called thee to do that which ye have inquired of me. Trust me for these things shall be made manifest before many. I will uncover their nakedness and their sin shall be made manifest. This I will do that they may acknowledge their wrong and repent. I have seen their wrongs and their sins are ever before me. I will cause their skirts to be turned back over their heads, yea they shall be shown; yea they shall be exposed. Many will marvel and others will weep at the wonders of my mighty hands. But it shall be for a sign unto my people. That they shall believe that I am He who blotteth out their transgressions; and remembers no more their sins.

To The Leaders:
I am weary with your oblations and offerings before me that are profane yea even a curse. A curse because even though you have been warned, you have continued in your way. I have blessed and yea do continue to bless; but yet you offer unto me that which is profane. Your hearts are evil before me; yea you do run swiftly to do that which is wicked and profiteth not my people; but rather that which flesh doth glory in, though I have told you that I will not share my glory with another.

To The People:
I have spoken in your midst many times concerning your sins; but yet ye say this word does not concern me, but another. I am speaking to the stout hearted men; not to the poor in spirit, not to the one of a contrite heart. I will warn you yet again. Your sins are before me continually. You tarry in your way; after your own desires and the desires of those who align themselves with the perverseness of your way.

Present all things honest in the presence of men. Turn from the commands of your heart and follow my commandments. This is my commandment that ye love one another that your joy may be full. Love, covers a multitude of sins. Seek forgiveness and repent of the evil that has been so long among you, lest ye die in your transgressions. Root out the evil; pluck it up and cast it out from among you; lest ye be as dead men walking.

Repent of the evil that is among you. Flush it out. In your present state ye are as cesspools before me; ye are profane; remove the profane thing. I will pardon; I will restore; I will renew. For I am plenteous in mercy; yea I will forgive. Let not your good be interred and obscured for the sake of the evil.

Jeremiah 4:1-2 (NASB)
"If you will return, O Israel," declares the LORD, "Then you should return to Me And if you will put away your detested things from My presence, And will not waver, And you will swear, 'As the LORD lives,' In truth, in justice and in righteousness; Then the nations will bless themselves in Him, And in Him they will glory."

Walk in the Light

I love you with an everlasting love. Seek me and live. Walk no longer in abomination. Seek peace with all men. Remember, my grace is sufficient for thee. I will renew, I will refresh, I will replenish. Seek me and live. Search for Me with all of your heart.

I have called you out of the darkness into the marvelous light of My Dear Son. Walk in the light; as you have received the Lord Jesus, walk in Him. H

John 8:12 (KJV)
12 Again Jesus spoke to them, saying, "I am the light of the world. Whoever follows me will not walk in darkness, but will have the light of life."

Watch Me

Watch Me! I will show thee great things. I am the Lord thy God. Watch me. Seek Me; yes, search after me. I will show you. Trust me. Lean not to your own understanding. In all your ways acknowledge Me and I will direct your paths. I will establish your goings; I will make your footsteps sure. Watch me, I say unto you.

I create both good and evil. The entire universe is subject to my will. I, the Lord declare it! I will move to set things right in your environment, in your home and among your brethren. I have seen the difficulties that you have faced as you tried to share My words with them.

No, they did not accept what you spoke, merely because it was the truth. I have set you among a people who will believe a lie rather than the truth. Do not worry or fret because of their faces and their harsh words. I will deal with them and they will know that you are My servant, whom I have sent to speak deliverance to them. I will bring them to their knees, as they bow down to seek my face for the turmoil that they are about to experience. I will do this even in your midst. For the Lord your God is mighty in your midst. Watch Me!

Exodus 6:2-12 (NLT)
2 And God said to Moses, "I am Yahweh—'the Lord.'* 3 I appeared to Abraham, to Isaac, and to Jacob as El-Shaddai—'God Almighty'* —but I did not reveal my name, Yahweh, to them. 4 And I reaffirmed my covenant with them. Under its terms, I promised to give them the land of Canaan, where they were living as foreigners. 5 You can be sure that I have heard the groans of the people of Israel, who are now slaves to the Egyptians. And I am well aware of my covenant with them. 6 "Therefore, say to the people of Israel: 'I am the Lord. I will free you from your oppression and will rescue you from your

slavery in Egypt. I will redeem you with a powerful arm and great acts of judgment. 7 I will claim you as my own people, and I will be your God. Then you will know that I am the Lord your God who has freed you from your oppression in Egypt. 8 I will bring you into the land I swore to give to Abraham, Isaac, and Jacob. I will give it to you as your very own possession. I am the Lord!' 9 So Moses told the people of Israel what the Lord had said, but they refused to listen anymore. They had become too discouraged by the brutality of their slavery. 10 Then the Lord said to Moses,
11 "Go back to Pharaoh, the king of Egypt, and tell him to let the people of Israel leave his country." 12 "But Lord!" Moses objected. "My own people won't listen to me anymore. How can I expect Pharaoh to listen? I'm such a clumsy speaker!

When God Speaks

In this world there are many voices and they each seem to somehow find their way into the corridors of your mind and interrupt your thought processes. Often, you may hear an inner voice speaking ever so softly, instructing, urging, prompting, or suggesting that you do or say a particular thing at a particular time. Sometimes, the voice seems so poignant, clear and precise; while at other times, you are left questioning whether you actually heard anything or not. Often you will ask; "is this you God, or is it my own inner voice that I am hearing?"

It was early Sunday morning and I awakened about 3:00 am (as I often do), but this particular morning was different. I was assigned to teach the Singles Ministry class at church. I had been given an outline from which to teach, however, the spiritual climate in the church during this season, was at an all-time low in regards to holiness and living in line with the Will of God. By the behavior of many of the young parishioners, it was apparent that blatant fornication and all out sin were the order of the day. The atmosphere in the church (in general), seemed to be riddled with complacency, compromise and indifference. It appeared that many of our single adults had resigned themselves to the adage that, "if it feels good, it's right." The Lord did not seem to fit into this picture at all. That morning, I was awakened by a voice that was instructing me to teach an unplanned, unscripted, lesson from Romans Chapter 1. Here, the Lord was pointing out His displeasure with the behavior of His people. Specifically, sexual sin and idolatry was rampant, so God laid out the prescription and the penalty.

Needless to say, much of the same was taking place in the local church, and of course, no one wanted to hear that taught on Sunday morning (immediately following the "good time that was had" on Saturday Night.) I really wrestled with the message and reasoned with myself regarding the specificity with which the command came. Needless to say, I questioned the Lord as to whether He was indeed speaking to me. His reply was given in parable form: "Yesterday, I walked with you where you are. Today, I look down upon you from where I am." I recognized it to be God. When God speaks, we must listen and obey.

Psalms 33:13 (KJV)
The Lord looketh from heaven; He beholdeth all the sons of men.

Psalms 33:14 (KJV)
From the place of His habitation He looketh upon all the inhabitants of the earth.

Speak To the Dead Things in Your Relationship

"You shall speak to the dead things in your relationship and they shall live again!"

Beloved, "I know that you are having a tough time finding the love, trust, and hope that you once had in your relationship; due to many people, places and things that have been allowed to creep into the corridors of your lives. That must cease – now!"
The Lord wants you to find your way back........to a place called "THERE" in your relationship. Let the Lord lead you; "for as many as are led by the Spirit of God, they are the Sons of God." Please do not harden your hearts, God is about to restore and rebuild what the enemy of your soul has tried to rob you of. Do not allow the enemy to steal your inheritance.

Psalm 147:3 (NIV)
"He heals the Brokenhearted and binds up their wounds."

Philippians 4:6-7 (NIV)
"Do not be anxious about anything, but in everything, by prayer and petition, with thanksgiving, present your requests to God. And the peace of God, which transcends all understanding, will guard your hearts and your minds in Christ Jesus.

Proverbs 21:30 (NIV)
There is no wisdom, no insight, no plan that can succeed against the LORD.

Areas that you may need to work on:
Being more involved with each other. Some relationships get stuck in merely existing under the same roof with differing views, without truly relating to each other. However, they pride themselves in respecting each other's interests and boast of non-interference in the affairs of the other. Some decide to do their best at "working together" for the sake of the children. While it

may seem stable on the surface, lack of involvement and communication increases distance. Then, when it becomes absolutely necessary to talk about something important, the connection, understanding and sense of understanding may no longer be there.

Resolving Conflict:
It is the choice of some couples to quietly discuss things and try to work out their differing opinions in an amicable fashion; while others may become loud and go ballistic if there is a disagreement of sorts. An important factor to developing a solid and effective relationship, is being able to face conflict head-on without shirking back. However, both must feel secure enough to be able to express their innermost thoughts and feelings with the other. It is imperative that there is a trust between them, to be able to do so without the formidable fear of retaliation lurking in the atmosphere. They must also be able to resolve conflict without humiliation, disgrace or the other insisting on being right, even when presented with indisputable evidence to the contrary. These folks have a need to massage their "ginormous" egos.

Remembering To Keep God Alive in the Relationship:
It is important that we understand that only God can satisfy our every longing. Expecting our mates to meet our every need is placing an impossible task upon them. Tending to place an individual on a pedestal and expecting too much from them can place that person in the very uncomfortable position of, bearing too much responsibility for the overall well-being of the relationship. This type of weight can be devastating in the long run. But with God, all things are possible. He is a burden bearer, skilled in carrying heavy loads and a friend that sticks closer than a brother. In the words of the older saints; "God is a burden bearer and a heavy-load carrier." Go on now and give it to Him!

Incorporating Basic Communication Techniques:

There is a certain look that one gives his/her mate that is clearly understood by both. You just know that look. This is body language at its best. Many feel that body language is probably the most powerful communication tool available to couples. It has been found that this works very well with children also. Do you remember snickering in church and receiving a certain look from your mother or grandma? You knew immediately that it was your queue to calm down and in some instances, it was a promise for greater things to come once church was over.

Reading body language is an excellent communication tool, which can ultimately instill a sense of trust and honesty. Even when we are silent, we are still communicating nonverbally. Often, the way you listen, look, move, and react tells the other person whether or not you care, if you're being truthful, and how well you're listening. We need to listen with our spiritual and natural ears so that we may gain the essence of what God is trying to convey in our relationship. So, we must stay "tuned in" to heaven so that we may hear his voice and gain direction.

You Will Live *and* Your Prophecy Will Work for You

Surely the Lord GOD will do nothing, but he revealeth his secret unto his servants the prophets. Amos 3:7 (KJV)

Believe in the Lord your God, so shall ye be established; believe his prophets, so shall ye prosper. 2 Chr. 20:20 (KJV)

It is the job of the prophet to do the following:

- *Reveal the nature and attributes of God to men*
- *Make known to men the laws of God*
- *Call the people back to obedience to God's laws*
- *Exhort the people to sincerity in worship*
- *Warn the people of Divine judgment upon sin, both personal and national*
- *Foretell future events which God had willed*
- *Foretell the coming of the Messiah, the Savior*
- *Record the history of God's dealings with men*
- *Record the Word of God in the Holy Scriptures*

Consider with me, the prophet Ezekiel. He was a shining example of someone who had been chosen by God and spiritually anointed with authority to speak into a situation for the purpose of beholding God's will come forth and manifest from the spiritual realm to the natural realm. In Ezekiel 36:21-24, Israel had been scattered and being the ultimate "shepherd, "it was God's will to bring them back together into their own land that they may serve and worship him.

Ezekiel 37:1-14 (NIV)
God tells Ezekiel to "speak to the dry bones that they may live:"

The Word of the Lord:

The hand of the LORD was upon me, and He brought me out by the Spirit of the LORD and set me in the middle of a valley; it was full of bones. He led me back and forth among them, and I saw a great many bones on the floor of the valley, bones that were very dry. He asked me, "Son of man, can these bones live?"

I said, "O Sovereign LORD, You alone know."
Then He said to me, "Prophesy to these bones and say to them, 'Dry bones, hear the word of the LORD! This is what the Sovereign LORD says to these bones: I will make breath enter you, and you will come to life. I will attach tendons to you and make flesh come upon you and cover you with skin; I will put breath in you, and you will come to life. Then you will know that I am the LORD.'"

So I prophesied as I was commanded. And as I was prophesying, there was a noise, a rattling sound, and the bones came together, bone to bone. I looked, and tendons and flesh appeared on them and skin covered them, but there was no breath in them.

Then He said to me, "Prophesy to the breath; prophesy, son of man, and say to it, this is what the Sovereign LORD says: Come from the four winds, O breath, and breathe into these slain, that they may live.'" So I prophesied as He commanded me, and breath entered them; they came to life and stood up on their feet – a vast army.
"I will put My Spirit in you and you will live."
God has spoken life to your dead situation and declares:

Psalm 91:14-16 KJV
14 "Because he hath set his love upon me, therefore will I deliver him: I will set him on high, because he hath known my name.

[15] He shall call upon me, and I will answer him: I will be with him in trouble; I will deliver him, and honor him.
[16] With long life will I satisfy him, and shew him my salvation."

The Mighty Releasing

Beloved, I am releasing a powerful anointing in this hour that will literally propel your faith to new heights. This anointing will be poured out upon those who dare to believe that I am a great and mighty God who longs to see my people prosper and be in good health.

You will begin to see occurrences that will literally set your mind to wonder with great amazement, even though it will be all too apparent to your senses. Yes, wonder and be amazed for I am releasing this anointing in proportions never before seen among men. You are about to see what heaven sees as I open your eyes with a new awareness.

Great and mighty healings will take place in this hour and many who have not known Me, nor experienced the depths of My love, will come running to Me. You will be My instruments in this hour and as you extend your hands, I will see your heart and release this great anointing upon you, which will cause men to marvel and be amazed.

So, extend your hands to heaven with a mighty shout of praise to your God and I will cause the walls of sickness, poverty and despair to come down with a great thunderous roar. Watch and be amazed as I release this great anointing in your day.

Ephesians 3:16 (NIV)
"I pray that out of his glorious riches he may strengthen you with power through his Spirit in your inner being,.."

Turn Your Face to the Wall

Dear Ones, these are indeed difficult times for many. It is time for My people to turn their faces to the wall and intercede for the multitudes. Many are experiencing needless pain and anguish, needless suffering and oppression, because they do not turn their faces to the wall. The picture that the world paints is bleak and morose. It brings many to the place of emotional unrest, which boarders on the fringes of mental depravity; all because they have not learned to turn their faces to the wall.

Did you not know that when you turn, immediately weights are lifted and chains broken and released? The Oppressor cannot stand in My presence. Turn your face to the wall, close out all surrounding clamor and seek Me My children. Come bearing the armor of God with a double-edged sword in your mouth. Speak My words that I have spoken over you, for they are spirit and they are life.

Speak the name of Jesus, for My name will bring water to your parched and dry land; it will bring healing to those whose bodies have been torn and ravished by the spirit of infirmity. It will bring relief and restoration to those who have been impoverished by living in a constant state of blindness, sin, rebellion, and denial. It will bring bread to the hungry, water to the thirsty and deliverance to the captives.

Seek My face. Come closer to Me. Turn your face to the wall so that you will not be able to see another. I want to show you who I am. Come closer My child; your life depends on it. Turn your face to the wall!

Isaiah 38:2 (KJV)
Then Hezekiah turned his face toward the wall, and prayed unto the Lord.

2 Chronicles 7:14 (KJV)
If my people, which are called by my name, shall humble themselves, and pray, and seek my face, and turn from their wicked ways; then will I hear from heaven, and will forgive their sin, and will heal their land.

Your Change Is On the Way

Beloved, you are faced with many problems that you feel there are no solutions for. Do not give up, your change is on the way. It is closer than you think. Often just when you are about to give up, you are at the brink of your breakthrough. The enemy of your soul has tried to lure you into a hopeless battle of the minds as you continue to be defeated by what the eye can see. I tell you that this is just another tactic to engender the spirit of doubt and hopelessness. These give way to unbelief and defeat.

You must always remember that no matter how difficult things may seem in the natural, I am always with you. Even when you are at your lowest, I am there. And just when it seems that you do not have the strength to stand, I reach out and hold you up, that you may not fall. When your strength is all gone, my perfect strength arises within you and suddenly you feel like going on. When all of your resources fail, it is then that I send My Angel of Provision to rescue you. I will never fail you.

Continue to look to me. Your change is eminent. I will bring forth a mighty restoration and renewal in your life and you will bless many. I call forth Change!

Matthew 7:7-8 (KJV)
Ask, and it shall be given you; seek, and ye shall find; knock, and it shall be opened unto you: For every one that asketh receiveth; and he that seeketh findeth; and to him that knocketh it shall be opened.

Disappointment

Do not be dismayed when others hurt and disappoint you. These minor afflictions are just what you need to assist with your growth. Disappointments are only temporary stumbling blocks which are often used as speed bumps along the highway of life. These bumps are used as instruments to remind you that you must slow down so that your travel along the highway of life does not become to you a racetrack of hurt, defeat, heartache and impending life-threatening danger. You must be reminded that you can do nothing without Me.

Too often My people do not seek the My Wisdom as they chart the course of this highway. To proceed on this highway without a roadmap, is a very dangerous endeavor; one which could cost very dearly.

My children, I stand ready to remove the speed bumps from your path, so that you may proceed on your journey with success in view. You must note that I have created you in My image and therefore you are filled with creative abilities which are waiting to be released. But the releasing of this great and marvelous gift comes by degree. When you move too quickly in your own will, you stand to veer off the straight and narrow highway and in so doing, you will head directly for spiritual and often physical destruction.

It is then that I place the greatest speed bumps in your path. I will never lose anyone that My Father has given Me. The problem with My children is that they become blinded with the lust of the eyes, the lust of the flesh and the pride of life, which causes them to desire the pleasures of "sin for a season" and risk missing the opportunity of acquiring life eternal with Me. Dear Ones, these choices bring disappointment to both you and me. You must remember the reason I died; so that you would escape the disappointment of hell for eternity. Each incident of disappointment brings forth growth.

Matthew 7:13-14 (KJV) *13 Enter ye in at the strait gate: for wide is the gate, and broad is the way, that leadeth to destruction, and many there be which go in there at:*
14 Because strait is the gate, and narrow is the way, which leadeth unto life, and few there be that find it.

Romans 5:1-5 (NASB)
1 Therefore, having been justified by faith, we have peace with God through our Lord Jesus Christ, 2 through whom also we have obtained our introduction by faith into this grace in which we stand; and we exult in hope of the glory of God. 3 And not only this, but we also exult in our tribulations, knowing that tribulation brings about perseverance; 4 and perseverance, proven character; and proven character, hope; 5 and hope does not disappoint, because the love of God has been poured out within our hearts through the Holy Spirit who was given to us.

Shore Up

Beloved, now is the time for you to shore up and leave no bases uncovered, no stones unturned. The enemy has sent forces out against you to attack your faith. You must turn your hearts towards me and pray like never before. This is no time to give in to the spirit of complacency and compromise. The enemy is sending a spirit of indifference which will cause many to surrender their battle attire and equipment.

Many have ceased from standing in the place of readiness. You must be ready at all times to enter into your strategic battle positions, shore up and prepare for war.

You will be unable to spring forth instantaneously if you are not totally armed and fully protected. This is a time of war. I am calling forth a Gideon's Army in this hour that will remain alert at all times, even when their heads are bowed down to the ground. This army will be in a state of watchfulness; ready to sound the alarm and warn of impending danger. I will prepare the battle ground; I will draw up the battle plans; I will go before this army and ensure their victory over the enemy.

In fact, I will cause a spirit of confusion and false illusion to come upon the enemy which will throw them into a state of panic. For they will reverse their efforts because of the great illusion and will begin to fight against each other to the extent of complete and overwhelming destruction.

Shore up! Awaken from your slumberous state. Put on your battle attire and go out to meet your enemy with confidence and assurance of victory. The Helmet of Salvation will protect your mind and bring your thoughts in line with mine. Your mind will begin to function on a completely higher and more profound level; for this helmet represents the mind of Christ. For divine protection, you will put on the Breastplate of Righteousness. For you stand complete in My righteousness and it shall be for you, protection of your spirit. The Shield of Faith will ensure that you stand strong knowing that I will establish whatever you decree. You have only to believe and stand on the authority of the name of Jesus.

Isaiah 59:17 (NKJV)
He put on righteousness like a breastplate, And a helmet of salvation on His head; And He put on garments of vengeance for clothing And wrapped Himself with zeal as a mantle.

1 Corinthians 16:13 (NASB)
Be on the alert, stand firm in the faith, act like men, be strong.

Section 4

The Watchman

Being

It is never too late to pursue your dreams and your gifts. Sometimes it feels as though you are sitting by the wayside watching the years as they pass you by, and yet your inner being is crying out for fulfillment. You gaze intently (as one mesmerized), at the beauty of the universe but yet you feel that you are in a vacuum, or somehow unable to connect with the ever evolving flow, of the very essence of the spatial expanse that surrounds you.

No, you are not disconnected, but rather connected to a more powerful source that moves deeply from within the essence of your being. You are familiar with this power and are able to draw from the very source of life that makes it finite, unquestionable, and absolute.

You have entered into a space where the source of being is larger than life and yet however, it is life. Your deepest wonderings begin to surface as mere incomprehensible nonsense, in light of the deep mysteries that are available and yours for the asking. Your spirit cries out with a resounding voice of praise and gratitude; to stand witness to such a deep and awesome experience.

Moving and riveting is the voice that you hear; booming like the sound of many rivers, as the response to your deepest yearnings and questions are so clear, precious and powerful.

"I am here with you and delight to share with you the mysteries of my kingdom. Come up higher so that the clamor of the universe will not distort your hearing. The words that I speak to you are unusual and will penetrate the deepest parts of your being; shattering all doubt, fear and unbelief. For the words that I speak are truth and life. Hold on to these words, as they will bring clarity and light to a world filled with darkness and lies.

Open your mouth and do not be afraid of the faces of those whom your words will most assuredly offend, for my glory will surround you and my presence will be your battering ram. You will break down the doors of sickness, addiction, marital and financial problems; social and emotional ills, and all other barriers to your success and the success of my people. Do not cringe, or shirk back because of uncertainty as to the course that you take, but rather trust in me to be your compass. The path will not always be clear but take the road that I show you and be sure to stay on course."

Mark 4:11 (KJV)
11 And he said unto them, Unto you it is given to know the mystery of the kingdom of God: but unto them that are without, all these things are done in parables:

What Do You Value?

What do you value? Where a man's treasure is, there shall his heart be also (Mt. 6:21).

Beloved, do not value worldly goods; for they will become old, useless and often worthless. Value the relationship that we had when we first met. Remember how much you loved me? Remember how you could hardly wait to be alone with me in our secret place? But when the blessings came, your love was poured out upon the things that you acquired as a result of our relationship.

You valued them more than Me. We met less often in our secret place. Your strength and anointing began to wane. You even began to become less selective of those who were allowed in your inner circle. Your eyes were completely turned on other things. My heart is broken for you. Come back and I will receive you; I will heal and repair your brokenness. Return to the one who values you greatly. I even gave My life that you may live.

Matthew 6:19-21 (ESV)
"Do not lay up for yourselves treasures on earth, where moth and rust destroy and where thieves break in and steal, but lay up for yourselves treasures in heaven, where neither moth nor rust destroys and where thieves do not break in and steal. For where your treasure is, there your heart will be also.

Matthew 16:26 (ESV)
For what will it profit a man if he gains the whole world and forfeits his soul? Or what shall a man give in return for his soul?

The Light

The darkness will be swallowed up by the light, for I will be in the midst. The darkness will be swallowed up for there will be light all around. Yea I will watch from My Holy Mount and yea, I will lift you higher. The barriers have indeed been broken and the strong holds have been torn down. Burdens have been lifted and yokes broken. The light has penetrated even the thickest darkness, and the bands of wickedness broken. Yea, even wickedness in the high places, even in the heavenlies.

I will do a new thing in the hearts of My people. I will mold them, yea, I will shape them and I will give them a new heart, yea, even a new mind. And they shall be My witnesses and they shall do great exploits. I will confirm My work with signs following. All shall know that I (the Lord,) am their God. They shall be mighty upon the earth and they shall be an army of strong men, even for the work of the Gospel. I will restore the hearts of men and I shall bring them to a place of safety in Me, saith the Lord.

1 Peter 2:9 (NKJV)
But you are a chosen generation, a royal priesthood, a holy nation, His own special people, that you may proclaim the praises of Him who called you out of darkness into His marvelous light;

Who Cares?

Imagine your mind taking a quantum leap into the dark abyss of terror and confusion. Imagine looking back (as you leap) only to see a shell that once housed your hurting soul; your shattered dreams and feelings of hopelessness and despair. You are falling rapidly into utter darkness, falling; falling; and yet with the last shred of your will, you fight to remain in the frame that once was you. You struggle to cry out for help, but even your screams are no longer the roar that caused you to proudly proclaim "I am woman hear me now because I have something to say." That demanding, take charge voice which ranges in modulation from the soothing hum of a lullaby to the screeching yelp of a lioness on the prowl; is suddenly reduced to a fearful whisper. But who cares?

Who cares when the lioness is wounded to the degree that she can no longer nurture, care for, and defend her young? Who cares? Who cared when one young mother was driven to the brink of utter despair and found herself in a position which caused her to give up her last shred of dignity and hope for a decent life for herself and her children, as she mulled over the decision made by the authorities, that she was no longer eligible for public assistance? Who cared when depression, fear, and trepidation took the last "piece of her mind," as she sat there alone in the darkness, shrouded in hopelessness, sorrow and grief?

Who cared when she tried to reach out but, there was no one there? Surely in this woman's mind, she was driven to the point of taking action to rectify the societal wrongs that were perpetrated upon herself and her children, at the most vulnerable time of her life. Where was the hand that should have been extended to this young grief-stricken widow, who was slipping further into that merciless black hole of life as each day went by?

Surely, you are not your brother's keeper, but the blood of her young are all over your hands. Where were the well-intended neighbors at the time that she needed them most? Someone must have noticed the red flag of distress that waved in the winds of the storm surrounding her dwelling. Surely, someone must have noticed when the merciless utility company discontinued her service.

Let us not forget our government's "feeding plan" for poor families. Surely, someone must have noticed that the United States Department of Agriculture (USDA) service had been discontinued to a young, needy family with no means of support. Our system is broken! Who cares?

Children missing from the school system, with no viable means or concrete plans to continue their basic educational requirements, and no hope for achieving their dreams or goals. No way out, hungry, starving, hurting, perplexed, fearful. Weakened emotionally, physically and spiritually broken. No future, not even a glimpse of a better world somewhere; anywhere. They wait, day after day; they just wait. "Perhaps someone will come and save me; rescue me from this loathsome condition." They wait in a cold, dark, dirty, row-house infested with vermin, vectors, disease-producing microbes and other predators; until death comes by, uninvited. They wait, but who cares? Then, it happens. She snaps and viciously takes the life of all of the children in the house.

Who cares? Surely not the system; that's clear. Where were the social workers, teachers, case managers, and others? Why did this tragedy have to take place? Who noticed the black flag of death waving over that dwelling during the period preceding the discovery of the bodies? Who cares?

What a travesty. What total neglect and lack of concern and compassion for humankind. We must forgive this woman and reach out to save her before another soul is lost; another life is taken away. What purpose does it serve to cast blame? Let the one within the system who is not responsible in some way for this shedding of innocent blood, be the first to cast a stone. The system is broken. Who cares? We cannot address the issues that caused this young mother to sink into oblivion and despair, by casting all of the blame on a poorly staffed workforce of whom, many themselves, may be moments away from slipping into the door of that black hole. Is termination of employment the answer? Who will replace those? How will they survive? Who will feed their children? Who will pay their rent/mortgages? Who cares?

Take notice city officials and other responsible parties, WE CARE! The system is broken! There is a hole in the dam! Fix it! Stop applying the "Band-Aid" and apply the "right aid!" Rebuild the system. Rebuild the city. Apply the Nehemiah Task to your urban renewal plans. Apply the "Master's Plan" to your social systems, your hearts. WE CARE!

Galatians 6:1- 10 (NIV)
¹Brothers and sisters, if someone is caught in a sin, you who live by the Spirit should restore that person gently. But watch yourselves, or you also may be tempted. ² Carry each other's burdens, and in this way you will fulfill the law of Christ. ³ If anyone thinks they are something when they are not, they deceive themselves. ⁴ Each one should test their own actions. Then they can take pride in themselves alone, without comparing themselves to someone else, ⁵ for each one should carry their own load. ⁶ Nevertheless, the one who receives instruction in the word should share all good things with their instructor. ⁷ Do not be deceived: God cannot be mocked. A man reaps what he sows. ⁸ Whoever sows to please their flesh, from the flesh will reap destruction; whoever sows to please the Spirit, from the Spirit will reap eternal life.

9 Let us not become weary in doing good, for at the proper time we will reap a harvest if we do not give up. 10 Therefore, as we have opportunity, let us do good to all people, especially to those who belong to the family of believers.

There Is Still Time

Beloved, in view of the many recent events that have taken place in the world's system, I encourage My people not to lose heart and to stand firmly upon the foundation that has been laid from times of old. Remember that your adversary does not win! He has deceived many into believing that he has power over them. However, all power belongs to Me. I am the sum total of all things. I am the Creator of the worlds and all that is within them. Every kingdom is subject to My great power. I have the power over all creation, over life and death, over all power in heaven, earth, and below the earth. I, and I alone, control all things.

Do not be unsettled by the occurrences that have surfaced in this hour. Did I not tell you that I would shake even the heavens and the earth; and that only the things which cannot be shaken will remain? Look unto Me; I am the same, I do not change. Come to Me; there is still time. Repent, turn and surrender the things which have held you captive, by exercising a spirit of deception over you for so very long. You are not defeated. In fact, you are more than a conqueror, for I have accomplished this for you.

Dare to believe what you cannot see. What I offer, you can only receive through the obedience of "belief." There is still time.

Ezekiel 7:7 (NIV)
Doom has come upon you, upon you who dwell in the land. The time has come! The day is near! There is panic, not joy, on the mountains.

Genesis 15:6 (NIV)
Abram believed the Lord, and he credited it to him as righteousness.

This Is My Prayer

Father, I want to do your will. Lead me with your out-stretched arm into your everlasting truth. Show me the perfect way; the perfect will of God and grant that I step into that place; the Perfect and Holy Will of God.

Father, my ability to love and obey is limited and incomplete. Help me simply to follow and not try to work it out or figure it out. Because the truth is, that you know my beginning and my ending and the course of my life is already laid out before you.

Lord, I desire to wait in obedience and to be totally surrendered to your will. Help me to see with Spirit Eyes, the path that you have designed for me to follow. Lord, I am ready and willing to be a "doer" of your word and not just a hearer. Strengthen me, help me to love your people. I desire to be more like you. Help me to see what you see in them.

I love you father. Teach me to love like you love. Show me how to love unconditionally. Remove the rough places in me. Lord, make the rough places smooth, and the crooked places straight. When I was down, you picked me up. When I was lost, you found me. When I was hurt, you comforted me. When I was sick, you healed me. When I was laden with sin, you forgave me. When I was in lack, you provided for me. When I was in danger, you rescued me. When I was hungry, you fed me.

I love you Father. I want so much to please you. Heal the areas of my discouragement and cause me to remember what you have done for me. Lord deliver my children. Make them whole again. Heal my family. I wait.

131

Psalm 23:6 (NIV)
Surely your goodness and love will follow me all the days of my life, and I will dwell in the house of the Lord forever.

Psalm 27:13 (NIV)
I remain confident of this: I will see the goodness of the Lord in the land of the living.

Psalm 69:16 (NIV)
Answer me, Lord, out of the goodness of your love; in your great mercy turn to me.

Gird Up Your Loins

Gird up your loins. This is not the time to retreat. Did I not tell you that the battle belongs to me? Even so, you must be fully armed and protected at all times. Your battle attire is a badge of distinction and you must wear it not only for protection, but also for connotation and as a symbol of recognition that you are of the army of the Almighty God. I have called you to a higher rank in this army. You will perform fearlessly and gallantly as you take position and know that you are of the army of Almighty God. I have called you to a higher rank in this army.

You will perform fearlessly and gallantly as you take your position and stand fearlessly against the ranks of demon forces that have been commissioned to attack you in every area of your life. I have called you to a higher rank in this army and equipped you with a mighty power, strength and anointing to accomplish the task. Preparation and execution are the key factors and are necessary strategies that will allow you to always be ahead of the enemy and not be shaken by his attacks. In preparation, you must always seek to "put on the whole armor of God," (remember this occurs in the spirit realm). Then execute your battle plan against the enemy which will paralyze his forces and cause them to flee in cowardice retreat.

Put on the mighty garments of praise and lift your voice in a song of praise, a shout which will cause the very mountains to shake and the seas to roar. A praise that will resound to the earth's core, piercing enemy forces with wounds which will cause them to scream and howl as they flee from my army. Lift up your mighty weapons of praise. As you sing My name, – "Jesus," the very atmosphere will change as the song that you shall sing begins to fill the air. I will cause your song that you sing, to increase in loudness in the atmosphere. Your song shall be a battle cry which will be heard by My Warring Angels and the heavenlies will be bombarded with the loudness of your shout unto Me. "Jesus!" Demons tremble, sickness must flee, situations change, the enemy is defeated when you say - "Jesus!" Say it with a mighty shout as you go forth. The name of Jesus shall be your mantra and you shall see the Jericho Walls in your life fall. This fall shall not be a fall in which the walls shall simply tumble over; but rather your battle cry has created a vast opening in the lower atmosphere and caused mountains to tremble; caused a tidal wave to violently form and sweep away all dirt and debris. This tidal wave shall not only be destructive waters, but healing waters; cleansing waters and waters which will soothe the parched and dry areas of your hearts, which have long awaited refreshing.

In ancient Hebrew times, both men and women wore flowing tunics. A belt or girdle was worn around the tunic. While tunics were comfortable and breezy, the hem of the tunic would often get in the way when a man was fighting or performing hard labor. So when ancient Hebrew men had to battle the Philistines, the men would lift the hem of their tunic up and tuck it into their girdle or tie it in a knot to keep it off the ground. The effect basically created a pair of shorts that provided more freedom of movement. Therefore, to tell someone to "gird up their loins" was to tell them to get ready for hard work or battle. It was the ancient way of saying "man up!"

Jeremiah 1:17 (NASB)
17 Now, gird up your loins and arise, and speak to them all which I command you. Do not be dismayed before them, or I will dismay you before them.

Job 38:1-4 (KJV)
Then the Lord answered Job out of the whirlwind, and said, 2 Who is this that darkeneth counsel by words without knowledge? 3 Gird up now thy loins like a man; for I will demand of thee, and answer thou me. 4 Where wast thou when I

laid the foundations of the earth? declare, if thou hast understanding.

Push Through – There Is a Winner in You

The race is long and the journey tiring, but the "Winner" must push through to completion. The twists and turns of life compels one to push forward, or otherwise be overcome by the many obstacles that crop up along the way. The way of the winner is difficult and requires perseverance. Never give up just because you are unable to see the finish line. Run your course and keep going, even when the end seems so far off. You will win if you do not quit. Your tired body is equipped with everything it needs to refuel and keep going, because you are fearfully and wonderfully made.

Know that you are more than a conqueror and nothing can keep you down. You are not in this race alone. Your help comes from the God who promised to never leave you, nor forsake you. You have to be in it to win it!

Push through in spite of the rough terrain, the insurmountable hills, and the long, winding roads. Keep your eyes on the prize. Push through the pain. Push through the hurt; push through the heartache and disappointment. You are almost there! Keep going until you make it, until you "break the tape" and reach the finish line.

Now you can see it! Faith has become sight! There is indeed a "Winner" in you. PUSH through!

1 Corinthians 9:24 (Amplified)
Do you not know that in a race all the runners run [their very best to win], but only one receives the prize? Run [your race] in such a way that you may seize the prize and make it yours!

Staging the Great Pretense

We are all performers and often do not show our true faces. Sin has caused us to lose confidence so we feel compelled to put on a disguise. There is a disguise for everything that you can imagine yourself to be. We don the "happy face" when we want the world to believe that everything is alright in our world. A façade can become the theatrical stage for development of the character that we really desire to be.

We enter the scene "stage left," all dressed in the costume that perfectly depicts just how we would like the world to think we truly feel. We step onto the stage, the curtains are opened, and we appear with the disguise that shows precisely what we are hiding. The disguise that truly covers us best, and becomes a perfect façade as we cowl in our hiding place. The disguise that is the direct opposite of our real feelings; and with this, we stage the award winning show! The characters are all real and convey with award-winning precision, the very counterfeit deceptive life-forces that we long to be delivered from, even though our clinging onto them, demonstrates a performance which appears to be quite the contrary.

- I'm perfectly happy
- Pride and Superiority
- Victim
- Indifference
- Bad Attitude
- Independence
- I Don't Care what you think of me
- Don't Waste My Time
- I Will Not Allow You to Control Me
- I'm Perfect in my Imperfections

We need to identify the types of situations that causes us to wear disguises in life; the ones that are more tempting for us to imitate. Which disguises are more useful for us in ministry? We must take a stand and let the enemy know that we are the "head and not the tail." We will not allow our feelings and fears to take control of our lives, but rather we will stand in the power of our God-given right to define how we live. We must stand in the power that Christ has given us and realize that we have power over the enemy! Jesus has given us "power to tread on serpents and scorpions." Therefore, we do not need to hide and cowl but rather take our predestined position in the Kingdom. Call on Jesus when the temptation to fake-it comes upon you. We must stop faking it; stop giving in and giving up. Just remember that God knows our every thought, and he hears us when we call. He is with us wherever we go.

Hebrews 12:1-2 King James Version (KJV)
1 Wherefore seeing we also are compassed about with so great a cloud of witnesses, let us lay aside every weight, and the sin which doth so easily beset us, and let us run with patience the race that is set before us, 2 Looking unto Jesus the author and finisher of our faith; who for the joy that was set before him endured the cross, despising the shame, and is set down at the right hand of the throne of God.

Thrust the Sickle In

Beloved, the Harvest is ripe and ready for gleaning. It is time to take up the instruments and begin to gather in the ripened crop. Many have labored and sown in tears and it is now time to reap in eternal joy and elation. The yield is great and there is much work to be done. The time for excuses has long since passed and now it is now time to rise up to the occasion, get to work and become doers, because the time is short. Many of you have tilled, watered, and prepared the soil of your hearts, so that the infallible word of God might fall on good ground. These are the days that the plowman will overtake the reaper.

Pick up your sickle and thrust in the blade, that you may be partakers in the plenteous harvest that is now ready for picking. We must gather this glorious harvest and the Lord will separate the wheat from the tares when He returns. Let us not be distracted, weary and tire now. We must be diligent to do this great work while there is still time.

Matthew 9:35-38 (NKJV)
35 Then Jesus went about all the cities and villages, teaching in their synagogues, preaching the gospel of the kingdom, and healing every sickness and every disease among the people.
36 But when He saw the multitudes, He was moved with compassion for them, because they were weary and scattered, like sheep having no shepherd.
37 Then He said to His disciples, "The harvest truly is plentiful, but the laborers are few. 38 Therefore pray the Lord of the harvest to send out laborers into His harvest."

Awaken From Your Stupor

The Lord desires to awaken His people from a Spiritual Stupor, which has spread, across this nation and is threatening to overtake the entire world. This stupor is far-reaching and penetrates the very psychosomatic core of mankind in such a manner that it changes the structural expanse of DNA located deep in the cellular structure of mankind, and seeks to re-make the very soul and spirit of man; defying the creative ability and finished work of Almighty God.

This deep far-reaching counterfeit change, has already made its stealthy claim to millions of Christians who are leaning and depending on the arms of flesh to carry them into the next move of God. This they do while remaining lazy, unfocused, and unprepared. Therefore, they become falsely unable to seek God for themselves.

Satan's lies have penetrated deeply into the church of God, making them believe a lie rather than the truth; causing them to place their hopes on a great harvest which they and their leaders are awaiting; but because of the blindness imposed by the God of this world, they are not be able to either recognize the harvest, or assist in any manner that would remotely resemble the appropriate response to God's current move.

Romans 11:8 (KJV)
(According as it is written, God hath given them the spirit of slumber, eyes that they should not see, and ears that they should not hear;) unto this day.

Deep Unabridged Worship - There is No One like Jesus

Beloved, the Lord is calling for Deep Unabridged Worship. We must give Him our all, (withholding nothing) and relentlessly pour out our heartfelt gratitude upon Him alone. He has prevented death from stealthy creeping into our lives during the night and extracting the very air that we breathe. He has given us an opportunity to share His love with others, so that they may indeed see our good works and glorify our God. For surely we will say of the Lord that He reached out and touched our deepest yearning, quenched our thirsty souls, healed our every longing and satisfied our needs. What's more, He gave us life, so rich and free.

My soul shall speak endearingly to Him on this wise: I love you Lord from the very depths of my being. You know me better than I know myself. You loved me when no one else would and crowned me with goodness and mercy. You are my provider, protector, my covering and my way maker. My lips shall never tire of singing your praise because my heart overflows with delight, knowing that you are my portion and my song.

I lay awake in the night watch meditating on your word, which brings me life and comfort. Your Wisdom is perfect and your precepts too marvelous for words. You are my refuge and my shelter during the times of storm. I do not fear the darkness of the valley because You are always with me. I do not feel the chill of the mountain air for You are my covering and my shield.

My soul longs for You and my spirit delights to answer when You call and rush to do Your bidding. My ears are attentive to Your voice and my feet spring quickly into dancing at the sound of your music. You hold my heart in the hollow of Your hands and provide my every need. Who is like unto You O Lord?

Exodus 15:11 (KJV)
"Who is like unto thee, O LORD, among the gods? Who is like thee, glorious in holiness, fearful in praises, doing wonders?"

Eternal

Are you willing to release all that you hold dear for one whose promises are so unclear? What is "eternal" life? How do we describe something so nebulous and mysterious? Yet the thought of it, in the context of "forever" seems somehow strangely intriguing.

In this world where there is always heartache, sorrow, insurmountable pain and suffering, the thought of a joyous escape to a place where opposites parallel the places and spaces in which we now live, seems indeed worth exploring. Over there, in the eternal, there is no more night, no more pain, no more sorrow, and no more tears. Instead the sun will shine brightly all day, every day. Where is this far-off sweet forever? Our Father would say:

"Why, it is here where I am beloved. Remember, I told you that in my father's house there are many mansions?" (John 14:2). The gates are made of the finest pearl and the main street of pure gold, so that you may always see the reflection of my glory all around you. Come away my beloved....eternity awaits....I will be calling you someday to "come away; come home" for you are eternal.

Song of Solomon 2:10 (KJV)
My beloved spake, and said unto me, Rise up, my love, my fair one, and come away.

I Am Raising Up a People

"I will no longer struggle with those whose hearts have become hardened by their sinful practices. I am raising Me up a people in this hour whose hearts have experienced a longing for Me. They have searched for Me with tears and repentant hearts. They have yearned to hear My voice and experience My closeness. I will tell you that this people that I am raising up in this hour, have withstood the test. They have come through the fire. They are prepared to go forth and become witnesses for Me. I have given them powerful, discerning spirits. They will be aware of every opposing force. They will be fully ready for Satan's attacks. They will be a people who are not ashamed of the gospel. They will lay down their lives for the sake of the gospel, like my servants of old.

I am raising up in this hour, the Spirit of Steven in My people, who will cry aloud, set the trumpet to their mouths and stand for holiness even unto death. I will cover My people whom I shall raise up from the shadows; even from every kindred and tribe; from every nation. I have placed a double edged sword in their mouths and a sickle in their hands. They shall be covered and arrayed with My Glory. The light of their countenance shall be a reflection for those who are walking in gross darkness and they shall find their way home. Do not fear, do not hesitate My Beloved. The time is short."

God is raising up the prophetic ministry in this last hour, to guide and warm His people (just as He sent prophets throughout history), to guide and warm His people. It is incumbent upon the people to listen and obey.

Deuteronomy 18:18-19 (NKJV)
I will raise up for them a Prophet like you from among their brethren, and will put My words in His mouth, and He shall speak to them all that I command Him. And it shall be that

whoever will not hear My words, which He speaks in My name, I will require it of him.

Joel 2:28 NKJV
And it shall come to pass afterward That I will pour out My Spirit on all flesh; Your sons and your daughters shall prophesy, Your old men shall dream dreams, Your young men shall see visions.

Romans 1:16 (NKJV)
For I am not ashamed of the gospel of Christ: for it is the power of God unto salvation for everyone who believes; for the Jew first, and also for the Greek.

I Am Waiting

My Child, I am here waiting for you. You must make time to seek My face and My righteous plan for your life. Do not allow ordinary hindrances to block your way as I will remove all stumbling blocks that have come before you to prevent you from meeting Me in our special place. Come away from everyone and everything that requires all of your attention and tires you out, so that even the least effort to meet me seems so difficult for you.

The enemy of your soul will not cease in his efforts to steal your purpose. You are needlessly pouring your energy into areas and things which have no recompense of reward in your life. Come unto Me all ye that labor and are heavy laden and I will give you rest.

Isaiah 30:18 (NIV)
Yet the LORD longs to be gracious to you; therefore he will rise up to show you compassion. For the LORD is a God of justice. Blessed are all who wait for him!

Isaiah 30:18 (KJV)
And therefore will the LORD wait, that he may be gracious unto you, and therefore will He be exalted, that he may have mercy upon you: for the LORD is a God of judgment: blessed are all they that wait for him.

The Lord Will Release the Captives

I am with you to bless you and ensure that you are safe from harm. I have built a wall of fire around you that will protect you from dangers seen and unseen. In this hour, there are many forces that have been sent forth to restrain and prevent you, but continue to forge ahead without fear or reserve and I will cause you to run through troops and leap over every wall of doubt, fear and unbelief. I will send you forth to be a formidable force to the netherworld as you move to obey My word and My will.

This is a time of release for My people. Too long have you been held captive by the tactics, ploys, plans, strategies and devices of the enemy!! I have come to set you free from hindrances that cause you to doubt your true calling. It is time for you to go forth and achieve the purpose for which you have been created and called. Yes, there is a divine appointment that awaits you in this hour. Many are waiting to be released from the prisons that have been erected in their minds, by spirits of anger, rebellion, bitterness and years of hurt and emotional pain. You will suffer no longer, for I am releasing you from the dungeons of despair, rejection, and depression and launching you to the heights of love, joy and peace! Go forth! Be strong! Darkness will flee in the light of My presence which is upon you!

Isaiah 61:1 (NIV)
The Spirit of the Sovereign Lord is on me, because the Lord has anointed me to proclaim good news to the poor. He has sent me to bind up the brokenhearted, to proclaim freedom for the captives and release from darkness for the prisoners.

In The Fullness of Time

Beloved, there is a time set aside for everything under the sun. A time for gestation and birth; a time to live, a time to die, a time for joy and a time for grief and sorrow. Nothing in the universe occurs before the fullness of time. There is a life-cycle for all things. The objective for My people, is to live their lives fully surrendered to My will and divine purpose. Then and only then, will their lives be fulfilled when death's final curtain is drawn on this earth and the spirit returns to Me.

Each man will give an account for the life lived in this earthly realm. I have given to each of you the necessary ingredients, to help you accomplish anything that you were assigned; the task of fulfilling your destiny and to soar to the next level of your purpose. Many of you have received and applied the training through study of My Word. In the fullness of time, when your work on earth is done, you will reign with Me eternally and experience unspeakable joy forever. Do all to see to it that you do not leave your work on earth undone.

Matthew 23:23 (KJV)
Woe unto you, scribes and Pharisees, hypocrites! for ye pay tithe of mint and anise and cummin, and have omitted the weightier matters of the law, judgment, mercy, and faith: these ought ye to have done, and not to leave the other undone.

Mark 8:36 (KJV)
For what shall it profit a man, if he shall gain the whole world, and lose his own soul?

Love

Love is a beautiful tapestry with each thread woven into the fabric of your lives.

Trust me today. Remove yourself from every obstruction, every hindering force that would interfere with your clearly perceiving and comprehending every word that you must receive from me. The day is coming when there shall be a famine of the Word in the earth. I will cause a deep hush to come upon the earth and I will not pity those who have become indifferent to My voice. Just as in the days of the Prophet Samuel, the Word of the Lord will be scarce. You may run to the false prophets who promote themselves by telling My people lies from the belly of hell, in order to promote their egregious words and lack of love for My people. Run as you may, but they will not be able to help you. Their words are empty and spawned from the annals of their wicked hearts. I will cover you with the blanket of My Love and open the ears of your hearts when you seek My face in love.

1 Corinthians 13:13 (NKJV)
13 And now abide faith, hope, love, these three; but the greatest of these is love.

1 Peter 4:8 (KJV)
And above all things have fervent charity among yourselves: for charity shall cover the multitude of sins.

Praise and Worship

To the Worship Leaders

Praise is an expression of heartfelt gratitude and thanksgiving to God for all He has done for us. It is a physical and vocal expression of our sincere appreciation to God for all of the wonderful blessings He has provided.

Worship is the highest form of praise. Going beyond the thoughts of all of His wonderful blessings to us, we are expressing our admiration and commending God Himself for His person, character, attributes and perfection.

Praise cannot hide disobedience! Just because we desire the presence of the Lord in our worship, it does not mean that we can do it "our way." The presence of the Lord must be ushered in as He leads, each time. The same tempo and order of songs that work this week, will not necessarily work next week. So let's be open to the Holy Spirit's leading.

John 4:24 (NIV)
God is spirit, and those who worship him must worship him in spirit and in truth (with our whole hearts)

Prov. 20:27 (NKJV)
The spirit of a man is the lamp of the lord, searching all the inner depths of his heart.

Rest

As Humans, we often tend to take on much more than we are capable of reasonably handling. Many of us are not aware that external demands can cause internal disturbances to our equilibrium and life-flow. When this occurs, it robs us of our innate ability to reason, causes undue stress and often leads to anxiety and a host of unsuspected ailments, from which we suffer with no concrete reason for their manifestation. Extreme tiredness, headaches, pain, nausea, insomnia, and a host of dermatologic issues are often attributed to stress.

It can be said that rest is, freedom from everything which wearies or disturbs our peace and security. The Oxford dictionary defines it as cessation from work or movement in order to relax, refresh oneself, or recover strength. Therefore rest is restoration, relief, and restitution. Rest requires a change in position and attitude. We need to know what time it is and understand that God very often will manipulate time and people in order to place you in the position that He wants you to be in. God has stored something up within you that will soon be released. Therefore, you need to position yourself to receive the blessings of the Lord in your life. However, every time God makes a move, the devil also makes a move.

Until now, you have yet to arrive at the place that God has appointed as your resting place; you have yet to come into your inheritance. Well, it is time that you cross over your Jordon and settle into your promised land. The minute you cross the Jordan River (figurative of decision) and settle into the land that GOD, (your God) is enabling you to inherit, He will give you rest from all of your enemies around about you.

God wants only His very best for you. Surrender your will and purpose yourself to come into His rest. This shall be a time of Rest; Restoration, Completion and Restitution!

Deuteronomy 12:10 (NIV)
10"But you will cross the Jordan and settle in the land the LORD your God is giving you as an inheritance, and he will give you rest from all your enemies around you so that you will live in safety.

Hebrews 4:1-3 NKJV
Therefore, since a promise remains of entering His rest, let us fear lest any of you seem to have come short of it. 2 For indeed the gospel was preached to us as well as to them; but the word which they heard did not profit them, [a]not being mixed with faith in those who heard it. 3 For we who have believed do enter that rest, as He has said:
"So I swore in My wrath, they shall not enter My rest, although the works were finished from the foundation of the world."

The Night Watch

Come My Beloved, you have work to do. The battle is raging and the attacks are becoming fierce. Keep watch during the night hours and do not faint. I have given you supernatural strength to endure the attacks and defeat the enemy. Listen to the voice of My Spirit, for in so doing, you will receive the strategy for victory. This present attack is fierce because your enemy is unsettled in his inability to destroy you. Do not give in nor give up! The victory is yours, for I have defeated your enemies.

Rise up with a new awareness of who you are. Did I not tell you that you are more than a conqueror? This is the hour that My people will rise to the standard of holiness that I have so long required. Holiness will be your banner as you march onto the battle field. You will defeat and bring to naught, all of the enemy's efforts to destroy your families, your finances, your relationships and your purpose.

I am sending you forth with a double-edged sword in your mouth, a praise on your lips, a battering ram in your hand, and a strong determination to defeat powers and principalities. Do not fear because I am with you to conceal and camouflage you so that you will no longer be a ready target; a sitting duck. You shall go forth with an electrifying energy that will emit shock waves throughout the universe. The world will know that you are My Army; My special forces that I have commissioned to destroy the enemy and deliver My people from bondage.

Take courage in knowing that My plan is tried, My way has been established. Get busy; there is work to do.

John 9:4 (KJV)
"I must work the works of him that sent me, while it is day: the night cometh, when no man can work.'

Advance

Beloved, now is the time for you to move out and step forward towards the goals that have been set for a very long time now. Although you have been obedient to your call, there is so much more that is awaiting your decision to simply Advance. You have only to move from the old familiar place and step out into the newly established horizon that has come about because of fasting, consecration, and as a result of prayers previously prayed. This is a time in which your faith will be lifted to higher heights and deeper depths. You have been given "great" faith and your reward will also be great. Do not allow fear, past failures, disappointments and hurts to hinder your progression. You must launch out into unfamiliar territories and uncover hidden places. As you launch out, you will use the power that has been placed within you to destroy the enemy's plans and expose and eradicate all of his tactics, schemes and devices. Your swift portability will allow you to step into preordained areas at any given time, where you will join forces with the Angels, to contend with and defeat spirits of infirmity and death. You will open blind eyes and set the captives free. Creation is waiting for you to Advance!

People of great faith will inherit the kingdom of heaven and be crowned with the crown of life as it is written, *"be faithful unto death, and I will give you the crown of life."*

Rev 2:10 (NKJV)
Do not be afraid of what you are about to suffer. I tell you, the devil will put some of you in prison to test you, and you will suffer persecution for ten days. Be faithful, even to the point of death, and I will give you life as your victor's crown.

Mt: 15:28 (NKJV)
Then Jesus answered and said to her, "O woman, great is your faith! Let it be to you as you desire." And her daughter was healed from that very hour.

Rev: 17:14 (KJV)
These shall make war with the Lamb, and the Lamb shall overcome them: for he is Lord of lords, and King of kings: and they that are with him are called, and chosen, and faithful

Exodus 14:15-16 (ESV)
Advance –go forward!
The Lord said to Moses, "Why do you cry to me? Tell the people of Israel to go forward. Lift up your staff, and stretch out your hand over the sea and divide it, that the people of Israel may go through the sea on dry ground.

Build Your Fences

I am calling for My people to erect fences, walls and fortresses around about them, that will prevent unwanted elements from entering in. The enemy will use every opportunity to interrupt your peace and bring confusion to disrupt and hinder you from your assignment on wall. You must "keep your heart with all diligence, for out of it spring the issues of life." Avoid distractions, idle tales, and too much talk.

Allow nothing to usurp your time as you must redeem the time, for it is short. But most of all, be careful to protect and safeguard your heart, for out of it flows the issues, storms, and challenges of life. Stand guard at the entrances and portals thereof.

The Fence-Line of My Life
God placed a wonderful saint in my life to be a fence around the things that He is building in me. She did not know that He used her as a safe-surround for my fragile and broken spirit. Broken in the household of faith. Misunderstood and mistaken in the world and a misfit in the system of darkness that once encapsulated my very soul. "You have been set apart," she would say. "You cannot have all things common with the people." You must separate yourself from the noise which disturbs the worshipper in you.

Yes, God had set a fence around me. A fence of protection; a fence of wisdom; a fence that would help distinguish and define His Holy calling on my life. The fence marked my space and prevented the intrusion of (fear, hurt, confusion and pain) and the disturbance of my spiritual equilibrium. A fence that would mark my territory and surround the boarders of my soul, how absolutely awesome!

Jeremiah 15:20 (KJV)
And I will make thee unto this people a fenced brazen wall: and they shall fight against thee, but they shall not prevail against thee: for I am with thee to save thee and to deliver thee, saith the Lord.

The Government Shall Be Upon His Shoulders!

I am calling my people to go forth with governmental authority to warn the nations!

"Then the seventh angel sounded: and there were loud voices in heaven, saying, 'The kingdoms of this world have become the kingdoms of our Lord and of His Christ, and He shall reign forever and ever!" (Revelation 11:15).

Jesus Christ—now seated at God's right hand—will come back to rule the nations of this earth as King of kings. We are told to think and meditate on what God is doing:

Colossians 3:1–4
"If then you were raised with Christ, seek those things which are above, where Christ is, sitting at the right hand of God. Set your mind on things above, not on things on the earth. For you died, and your life is hidden with Christ in God. When Christ who is our life appears, then you also will appear with Him in glory."

Verse after verse in the Bible shows that God will restore His government, His law and His way of life to this entire earth.

1 Thessalonians 4:16–17 (KJV)
"For the Lord Himself will descend from heaven with a shout, with the voice of an archangel, and with the trumpet of God. And the dead in Christ will rise first. Then we who are alive and remain shall be caught up together with them in the clouds to meet the Lord in the air. And thus we shall always be with the Lord"

In our mind's eye, we should picture the glory of Christ's return as King of kings—the great shout of the archangel's voice announcing the arrival of Earth's Sovereign Ruler, and the mighty blast of the Last Trumpet! When Christ returns, the above verse says that we will be "with the Lord." So where will that be? "The time of sorrows has begun, and My people have been caught up in a web of complacency, indifference, compromise and lack of consistency in prayer. Now is the time for My people to stand and choose whom they will serve."

Handle Your Sword with Care

Beloved, have I not told you that you must study to gain my approval and assure that you share my Holy Word with accuracy? My Word has more power than even a double-edged sword which has the ability to separate that which is useful, from that which is reprehensible and immoral, with "one fell swoop." Therefore, careful and considerable handling is in order.

The blade of your sword must be carefully maintained, so that it is always sharp and remains battle-ready. Do not use it foolishly and it will serve the warrior in you well. Because your sword is a dangerous weapon which has the capability of inflicting powerful death blows of truth to destroy the enemy and bring victory to the warrior, do not use it haphazardly and swing it through the atmosphere as if you were fighting a Hollywood dual.

But rather, handle it skillfully, with care and precision. You must value its worth. It has the ability to subdue enemy armies, confound them and send them running in terror.

Ezekiel 21:9-11 (ESV)
9 "Son of man, prophesy and say, Thus says the Lord, say: "A sword, a sword is sharpened and also polished, 10 sharpened for slaughter, polished to flash like lightning!
(Or shall we rejoice? You have despised the rod, my son, with everything of wood.) 11 So the sword is given to be polished, that it may be grasped in the hand. It is sharpened and polished to be given into the hand of the slayer.

Lord When Will It Be My Time?

You are always in a place where it seems that you are looking on. However, you know that there is something within you that is waiting to be manifested and somehow you feel that you are in the wrong position. As you stand within yourself and look out from yourself to the place that you find yourself in, you know that you are not in the right position. Why are you always the one who is somehow assisting others to climb to their plateaus and yet when your time comes there is no one there to assist? Why does it seem that you are always alone, accept when you are surrounded by those who desire that you use your God-given talents to elevate themselves?

Have you found yourself in this position all too many times? Do friends seem to walk away just at the time you seem to need them most? Is it difficult to always be the onlooker when you know that there is a place that God has prepared somewhere for you? Then allow me to share with you today, that God is about to release that which has been stored up in you. You have served your time in the right position beloved; a position of "waiting on the Lord." The issue is that God has an appointed time for each of us to emerge from the waiting room.

The Apostle Paul explains in Romans 12:7-9; that we must wait in a "holding position" for God to put the finishing touches on our ministry, until the conclusion of the maturation process:

"Having then gifts differing according to the grace that is given to us, whether prophecy, let us prophesy according to the proportion of faith; Or ministry, let us wait on our ministering: or he that teacheth, on teaching; Or he that exhorteth, on exhortation: he that giveth, let him do it with simplicity; he that ruleth, with diligence; he that sheweth mercy, with cheerfulness." (KJV)

161

Our Father may also allow us to remain in the holding position until we learn to turn our eyes upon Him and refocus our attention. In other situations, God may have us to wait, because the timing is not quite right to give us the......"Go Ye." Perhaps certain events must happen first, or our thinking may need to change. There are also seasons when the Lord wants to stretch and grow our faith.

The Shifting is About to Take Place

Finally, while you are waiting, often the Lord is building you up for the task at hand. Or, He may be setting other people, places and things in the right position so that your transition from the waiting room to the delivery room will be smooth.

So rest assured that according to the word of the Lord;
"You have dwelt long enough at this mount; Go in and possess the land!" Deuteronomy 1:6, 8 (KJV)

Beloved; "continue steadfast, immovable, ever abounding in the work of the Lord." This is your time! Step into it and embrace the moment. It has been a long time coming.

The Prophet Habakkuk says:
"For the vision is yet for an appointed time; But at the end it will speak, and it will not lie. Though it tarries, wait for it; because it will surely come, It will not tarry."
Habakkuk 2:3 (KJV)

Taking the Next Step - *My Darkest Hour*

Where do I go from here? How do I strategize my next move? Have I planned or chartered the course of my life's direction? Have I sought God's direction? Did I follow his lead? Many seem to think that I have it all together however, as for me, I feel that there are so many ways that I could go and I just need to narrow them all down, so that I may see my way clearly.

I've never liked the untold story, groping in the darkness, or the unfinished chapter. Now I have come to the very place that I've somehow looked forward to for so long. Now that I am here, I don't know where to go, or rather, how to get started with the rest of my life. One day, I suddenly found myself thrust into a situation that, although I knew it would come, I was not quite ready for the way in which it came. Suddenly...no time to think or plan for what should have been a smooth transition.

The love of my life, my husband and long-time best friend, was suddenly diagnosed with the dreaded disease......*cancer*. At that very hour, the tapestry of my life seemed to somehow be coming apart at the seams, and I was left to hold on to the threads before they all unraveled. What a task! What an enormous blow to the very core of my existence, my soul was numb, frozen, stunned, and without emotion. My world began to reel tighter and tighter until I could hardly breathe; but breathe, I must. This is why my husband "found me" as the word of God states, *"he who finds a wife, finds a good thing and obtains favor from the Lord." Proverbs 18:22 (NKJV).*

God's plan was about to become unveiled in a most tangible and awesome way. But again, my first question was, "what I am I going to do? Where must I go from here? When these things happen we are always so very much unprepared and there is no manual to follow. However, there is one thing for sure; when life's tragedies suddenly arise, we must look to *Jesus, the author and the finisher of our faith.* Look to Him, draw near to Him and above all, follow His lead. He will show you the way.

Psalm 46:5 (KJV)
God is in the midst of her; she shall not be moved: God shall help her, and that right early.

The Time of Enlightenment

Beloved, do not feel bewildered and sad when adversity comes your way. Rejoice, in that you will see the hand of God move firsthand, as I set in order that which is in disarray. Let your faith become sight and see Me reveal My power in your midst. Did I not tell you that *"in this world you will have tribulations, but be of good cheer for I have overcome the world? (Jn. 16:33)*. Let your faith work for you and see you through these difficult situations. It is My desire that you grow stronger as you soar to heights unknown.

Your transition into your destiny will take on new speed as you move quickly through one level of awareness to another. The time is short and you have less time than ever before. So redeem the time and seek My face all the more, with a longing that surpasses any other period during your lifetime. You will draw closer to Me in prayer, and our time together will be a time of preparation and strengthening.

Those who diligently seek Me will find the treasure of life reserved for the children of the kingdom. Be committed to prayer and fasting; make your requests known and have confidence that your prayers will be heard even before you ask. I will send signs and wonders during these times to assure you of My love for My people. I will save, restore, heal and bless my people so that their hope is no longer deferred. This time shall be called the time of "enlightenment."

Micah 7:8-9 (KJV)
Do not rejoice over me, O my enemy Though I fall I will rise; Though I dwell in darkness, the LORD is a light for me. I will bear the indignation of the LORD Because I have sinned against Him, Until He pleads my case and executes justice for me He will bring me out to the light, And I will see His righteousness.

Ephesians 1:18 (NKJV)
I pray that the eyes of your heart may be enlightened, so that you will know what is the hope of His calling, what are the riches of the glory of His inheritance in the saints,

Whirlwind

You are in a whirlwind of mindless cerebral motion and there seems to be no end to the trajectory of thoughts that are surfacing. Did you not know that as a man thinketh in his heart, so is he?
(Pr. 23:7) Aberrations of images from the past (people, places, and things), continue to dance around in your mind as if it were a kaleidoscope playing on a jumbotron, somewhere in a vast cavernous spacial expanse, in the middle of nowhere.

The problem here is, that you must let go of the past and move on, *"forgetting those things which are behind" (Philippians 3:13)*, clearing the path for new dreams, visions and relationships. You must be especially careful to deny access to all invaluable thoughts that creep into the corridors of your mind, threatening to prevent you from accomplishing your God-ordained purpose.

Where is this place? It all seems strangely dim somehow. You pant for breath, longing to hold on to some semblance of what is called a sense of normalcy however, you are completely immersed in this entire scene. Your inner voice cries out "let it go." It is at this very moment in time that you must be willing to let go of anyone or anything that threatens your wellbeing. Strangely enough, you often make excuses for holding on to your "idols," though you are emphatic in your renunciation of their lingering existence in your thoughts. "Let it go!"

Why would you pamper the devil? Prepare the death certificate for old relationships, people, places and things that no longer serve a purpose in your life. Close the door on old thoughts, dreams and ideas that will only result in reprehensible damage to your inner self and no longer have purpose or meaning in your life. "Let it go!"

Let the breath of God blow new life upon the areas of your heart and mind that are preserved for God and God alone. My child, I still "know the plans that I have for you".....look for the future that I have promised you and you will find that it is closer than you can imagine. BELIEVE...I will bring it to pass in even a short time. I will blow my wind upon your life and you shall know that it is I. Know that I will not share My Glory with another, for I am jealous for you.

Ezekiel 37:8-10 (KJV)
And I looked, and behold, sinews were on them, and flesh grew and skin covered them; but there was no breath in them. Then He said to me, "Prophesy to the breath, prophesy, son of man, and say to the breath, 'Thus says the Lord GOD, "Come from the four winds, O breath, and breathe on these slain, that they come to life." So I prophesied as He commanded me, and the breath came into them, and they came to life and stood on their feet, an exceedingly great army....

Worry

Beloved, can you change your situation by fretting or worrying? Trust Me. I will walk with you through the darkest and most foreboding clouds, and I will cause the darkness all around you to flee. I will cause you to ride upon the storms of life, as I use each gruesome situation that confronts you, to fill you with an insurmountable strength that will cause even mountains of fear and doubt to move as I bring about a change in your innermost being. It is also during these times when the enemy would desire to fill you with fear and worry that I will cause your spirit to arise and peer into the very center of My heart. Cease from worrying and allow me to work it out for you. Worry is tantamount to doubt and unbelief.

Matthew 6:27 (KJV)
Which of you by taking thought can add one cubit unto his stature?

Proverbs 12:25 (NKJV)
Anxiety in the heart of man causes depression, But a good word makes it glad.

James 1:5-8 (NKJV)
5 If any of you lacks wisdom, you should ask God, who gives generously to all without finding fault, and it will be given to you. 6 But when you ask, you must believe and not doubt, because the one who doubts is like a wave of the sea, blown and tossed by the wind. 7 That person should not expect to receive anything from the Lord. 8 Such a person is double-minded and unstable in all they do.

Heart - Cry

I hear your *heart-cry*. I know what you need even before you ask, says the Lord. And, I am with you and leading the way, but you must yield yourself completely to Me in total faith and trust that I will direct your steps. Relinquish all that worries you. My ways are higher than your ways, and I will do what is ultimately best for you spiritually. Put yourself in My hands, and I will take care of you. *"Which of you by worrying can add one cubit to his stature?" (Matthew 6:27)*

You need to examine your heart to determine what lies you have believed. These lies may not be anything that you have heard, but rather what you have observed. And the lie has created an open door for the spirits of fear, infirmity, and heaviness. You must bind these devils and begin to rebuild your faith by reading My word. You need truth to bring light to this place of darkness, says the Lord.

2 Timothy 1:7 (NKJV)
For God has not given us a spirit of fear, but of power and of love and of a sound mind.

Choose Me

Beloved, there are so many choices in life, but it is important to understand that you have been created to make your own choices. You have been fearfully and wonderfully made to carefully and strategically plan and decide what your portion shall be. I beseech you to choose Me today and live your best life, while you are on this tedious journey.

In life, there are so many choices. Many of them are channeled by the enemy of your soul to bring pain and despair; to interfere with your relationship with Me. However, My Beloved, the choice is yours to make. I implore you to choose Me. For you see, *in My presence is fullness of joy; at my right hand there are pleasures forevermore.* I long to bless you because I alone know the plans that I have for your life; your purpose. I will bring you to a place of accomplishment in your future endeavors.

Choose Me, because I alone know your beginning from your end. Your emotions cannot be exchanged for a transitory euphoric moment of ease. I came to bring you peace and abundant life. Your hurt and pain cannot be removed by a temporary perversion and misrepresentation of the eternal; but merely lifted for a fleeting moment. Choose Me. The one who gives you eternal, never-ending life, love and joy unspeakable. Choose Me.

Jeremiah 3:14 (NASB)
Return, O faithless sons,' declares the LORD; 'For I am a master to you, And I will take you one from a city and two from a family, And I will bring you to Zion.

A Change Is Coming Today

The number 14 represents deliverance or salvation and is used twenty-two times in the Bible. The term "14th" is found 24 times in scriptures. The fourteenth day of the first month is the Passover, God delivered the firstborn of Israel from death.

God made two covenant promises to Abraham — one of the physical seed, Isaac, and his descendants, and one of the spiritual seed, Jesus Christ, and the sons of God who would come through Him, who would *shine like the stars of heaven (Matthew 13:43)*. On the day portion of the 14th, God confirmed the promises with a special covenant sacrifice. It also marks the conclusion or ending of a matter. It is time to close the door! Enough is enough! It is time to close the door on some things in our lives. (Such as):

People – who mean us no good
Places – we should leave behind
Things – we should get rid of
Habits – we should break
Lifestyles – we should adjust/change
Attitudes – we must change
Issues – that keep us from hearing from God
Lack – God shall supply all of your needs
Bad debts – repay them
Bad decisions – repent/refrain; *do not allow wisdom to take a back seat*
Lack of commitment – be steadfast, immovable and trustworthy
Fooling around with the things of Almighty God – return to your first love

2 Corinthians 5:17 (ESV)
17 Therefore, if anyone is in Christ, he is a new creation. The old has passed away; behold, the new has come.

Psalm 51:10 (ESV)
10 *Create in me a clean heart, O God, and renew a right spirit within me.*

Section 5

28 Days of Prayer and Praise

Day 1 - What Shall We Do?

John 6:28(NKJV)
28 Then they said to Him, "What shall we do, that we may work the works of God?"

Here we are once again, bound together by the love that only the immutable, omnipresent, omniscient and omnipotent God of our fathers (and the Lord Jesus Christ), has by His sovereign power ordained us to carry on the "Greater Works" Ministry, while today is still called today. I thank God for each of you and I am honored and proud to call you "family."

We bless God and give Him honor for ordaining us to stand in the gap and make up the hedge around about the Hands of Love Missionary Leadership, the U,S. Missionary Team to Uganda, the Host Clergy and ministerial teams, conference speakers, the people of Uganda, the women and children of Uganda, again this year.

We link our spirits together with the many intercessors who have been likewise ordained to this great work, and we pray that the "Spirit of Unity, Love and Peace" would help us to operate in the realm of the "Holy Spirit" boldly and without compromise.

Humble us Dear Lord, and cause us to lay aside every hindrance; encumbrance; obstacle; and the besetting weight of sin that may have crept into the gates (corridors of our hearts and minds). Humble us, so that Your Mighty anointing would begin its work of deliverance and reformation right at this very hour. Let it begin with us, with your missionaries, your servants, even before the plane lands safely in Uganda. Provide for every need, bless the "hands" that are so willingly extended to minister to the needs of Your people.

We boldly come in collision with the territorial hosts of hell in Uganda and subsequently bind Powers, Principalities, Spiritual Wickedness in High Places and render them ineffective in their plans, plots and schemes against this work, in the Name of Jesus! Every strong man is bound, and every dark covenant broken.

We pray that the Lord would assign His angels that excel in strength, to go forth and provide protection for each of you every minute of every day. We bid you traveling mercies, in the name of Jesus; Amen!

Day 2 - God's Favor Is Upon You; *Strength To Survive The Storms*

Isaiah 43:2 (NLT)
When you go through deep waters, I will be with you.
When you go through rivers of difficulty, you will not drown.
When you walk through the fire of oppression, you will not be burned up; the flames will not consume you.

The Message (MSG)
When you're in over your head, I'll be there with you. When you're in rough waters, you will not go down. When you're between a rock and a hard place, it won't be a dead end—

Beloved, you are a SURVIVOR! But God's Divine Favor is upon you. Did you know that your favor is infectious? Yes, because of the favor on your lives, others will be blessed. You must know and believe that despite the storms, difficult times, the trouble and the bondage that you, (yourself) may have suffered or experienced, God will use you to bless those to whom he sends you – as broken as you are.

So, in spite of all that comes your way, just know that if God gives you a promise, He will show you favor in the midst of it all; until that promise is fulfilled.

So your job may be going thru changes, but God will show you favor! Your relationships may not be what you would like them to be; but God will show you favor. People may be acting funny toward you in your time of need; but God will show you favor with a stranger to help preserve you! You have the Favor of the Lord; and that makes you a survivor!

Day 3 - Release - Do Not Hold Back!

Zechariah 4:6
So he said to me, "This is the word of the Lord to Zerubbabel: 'Not by might nor by power, but by my Spirit,' says the Lord Almighty.

The Message (MSG)
"This is God's Message to Zerubbabel: 'You can't force these things. They only come about through my Spirit,' says God-of-the-Angel-Armies. 'So, big mountain, who do you think you are? Next to Zerubbabel you're nothing but a molehill. He'll proceed to set the Cornerstone in place, accompanied by cheers: Yes! Yes! Do it!'"

Dear Ones, My Spirit shall be a "canvas" of protection over you. So do not be reluctant to release the treasures from within. Remember, I have already sent My Word to heal and delivered them. So, the fundamental cursory work has already been done. You have only to allow your inner man to break through the obstacles and hindrances surrounding your outer man. Sometimes these hindrances have been strategically perpetrated by the enemy of your soul, in order to block your success. However, you must be clear, that the first obstacle to your work is yourselves, not other things.

I am extending a mighty surge of My "Dunamis Power" that will supply even the greatest need. When you step aside and allow Me to totally dismantle your broken outer man, you will become a conduit for My power. Many will come and regain their strength; sinners will be saved; many will be healed; the lame will walk again; deaf ears will hear; blind eyes will regain their sight; broken hearts will be mended and the prodigals will return. Move boldly and do not hold back; for I have imparted to you, power to "Release!"

Day 4 - The Mountain of His Presence

Isaiah 25:6-8 (NIV)
On this mountain the Lord Almighty will prepare a feast of rich
food for all peoples, a banquet of aged wine, the best of meats
and the finest of wines. ⁷ On this mountain he will destroy the
shroud that enfolds all peoples, the sheet that covers all nations;
⁸ he will swallow up death forever. The Sovereign Lord will
wipe away the tears from all faces; he will remove his people's
disgrace from all the earth. The Lord has spoken.

Revelation 5:9-10 (NKJV)
...⁹ᵇ For You were slain, And have redeemed us to God by Your
blood
Out of every tribe and tongue and people and nation, ¹⁰ And
have made us kings and priests to our God; And we shall reign
on the earth."

Beloved, Everything the Lord is doing in these last days, is closely tied to his Presence. God is calling you to "come up higher," even to His Holy Mountain. This is a special place in the very Throne Room of Heaven; where the Spirit of the Lord is manifest. It is a holy place; the "Mountain of His Presence." It is a place where we go to commune and sup with Him, worshiping Him in spirit and in truth.

In fact, the Mountain of God is where the throne room is in heaven. When we live as kingdom priests (Rev 5:10), the Top of the Mountain_of the Lord is where we present ourselves before Him. Everything the Lord is doing in these last days, is closely tied to his presence. This "Mountain of God's Presence" is an important consideration for us today; and His feast of fat and wine can only take place where Jesus' presence is manifest.

God has predestined you for this work. So even though you may be different, and at different stages in your growth, God is trying to lead all of us to the same place. So, just set your heart to believe what your mind cannot conceive; and He will bring it all to pass. Rest assured that He is with you and will show Himself Mighty in your midst. Simply stated, whenever Jesus makes himself known, everyone present senses it. Every spiritual wall and fleshly stumbling block evaporates when Jesus makes himself known!

In fact, Christ's presence is so real when it is manifested; you can almost touch it! It is His desire to work amazing miracles in your midst that will first, overwhelm your minds and hearts; and then those of the people. He planned it all even before the world existed. If He has devised such a covenant plan, then it must and will happen. Welcome to the Mountain!

Day 5 - The Glory of God Is Upon You

Romans 10:13
"Whosoever will call upon the name of the Lord will be saved."

Dear Ones, even though the earth is full of God's presence and glory, many do not perceive it. Look at (Deuteronomy 5:24-27):

"The Lord our God has shown us his glory and his majesty, and we have heard his voice from the fire. Today we have seen that a man can live even if God speaks with him. But now, why should we die? This great fire will consume us, and we will die if we hear the voice of the Lord our God any longer. For what mortal man has ever heard the voice of the living God speaking out of fire, as we have, and survived? Go near and listen to all that the Lord our God says. Then tell us whatever the Lord our God tells you. We will listen and obey "

When glory comes down, it's a bit of Heaven's atmosphere coming down to us, a taste of His Manifest Presence." As His glory increases by degree, there might be healings or other manifestations exhibited. In His presence, we begin to see ourselves for who we truly are. We begin to realize that we are one French fry short of a "happy meal" in His presence and immediately begin to repent and seek His forgiveness. His glory brings about a change in our relationship with Him, with others, and there is even a visible change in our appearance, our (countenance). At this present time the Lord is raising (us) up, a body of spiritual beings who will bear His glory, and not only bear it, but will even be on the throne with Him. We are learning what the cherubim have known for ages. We are learning to function in unity just as the cherubim and the four living creatures functioned in bearing the throne of God and carrying His glory. When we are perfected in unity, the world will marvel. God's glory is upon you; all around you. Bask in His glory!

Day 6 - Do Not Abort the Baby

Jeremiah 1:4-6 –
Then the word of the Lord came to me, saying: "Before I formed you in the womb I knew you; before you were born I sanctified you; I ordained you a prophet to the nations." Then said I: "Ah Lord God! Behold, I cannot speak, for I am a youth." But the Lord said to me: "Do not say, 'I am a youth,' for you shall go to all to whom I send you, and whatever I command you, you shall speak."

Are you spiritually pregnant with God's seed? Have you grown weary during the developmental process of the promise or vision that you have been carrying on the inside? If so, I have good news for you today.

I believe that many of God's people are pregnant with God's promises. The birthing of these promises are close at hand. Don't allow the enemy to come in and abort the baby! It is time for the body of Christ to cut out the negative talk that we somehow immerse ourselves in. Our negativity has the capability to abort the spiritual promises that are being developed in the womb of our spirits. We must stop speaking negative words over our promised seed. We must align ourselves with God's will in order to birth what He has placed on the inside of us. If we fail to do this, we will suffer the consequences of our disobedience. It doesn't matter how old or how young a person is when God begins to speak His word into them.

The words, "I cannot," should not be included in our vocabulary. When the Lord tells us to do something, it means that He has already equipped us to accomplish the command. When we respond to His command with, "I cannot," we are positioning ourselves for a spiritual abortion. God's promises are so much bigger than our finite minds can comprehend. This is why

Scripture declares, "The just shall live by faith." The just shall not live by doubt and unbelief. Faith supersedes the natural. Faith speaks to those things that are not as though they were. Faith says, "Yes and amen," when God speaks. Faith causes God's seed on the inside of us to grow to maturity. Faith walks us through the birthing process and delivers the promises of God. Do not Abort the Baby!

Day 7 - Hearing God

We hear on multiple dimensions. We must have an ear to hear.

Father, as a secondary consequence of our worship, speak to us O Lord. Not from the outer court but from the inner court. Feed us; not with milk, but with meat. In Jesus' Mighty Name – Amen.

One of the greatest blessings a true believer has ever experienced, is to hear and know the voice of God. It is possible to hear God's voice today as certainly and clearly as did Abraham and Moses; as clearly as did Samuel and David; as clearly as did Paul, Peter, the apostles and John on the isle of Patmos! God has promised to make His voice clearly known for one last time during these end days. He has given us a promise and a warning about hearing His voice. God is going to bring together a holy, separated remnant into spiritual Zion and make His voice known to them.

"But ye are come unto mount Zion, and unto the city of the living God, the heavenly Jerusalem, and to an innumerable company of angels" (Hebrews 12:22).

God has this message for all who have been called out to do this marvelous work in Uganda:

The voice of God that has shaken the earth in past generations will be heard in power again, in one last shaking!

26 *"At that time his voice shook the earth, but now he has promised, "Once more I will shake not only the earth but also the heavens." (Hebrews 12:26)*

Here is God's warning to His holy, believing children:

25 "See to it that you do not refuse him who speaks. If they did not escape when they refused him who warned them on earth, how much less will we, if we turn away from him who warns us from heaven?" (Hebrews 12:25)

God's voice is heard only by those shut-in with Him in secret prayer. God is very careful to whom He speaks. It is only to those who value His voice so much that they shut the whole world out, to get alone and wait for Him.

When we refuse to discipline ourselves to be alone with God to hear His voice, we become strangers to that voice. We are not strangers but daughters and sons. He longs to speak with you. He has so much to tell you. Listen and expect to speak forth the words that He gives you for His people. Prophesy what you hear. "Today, you will prophesy to the four winds;" the Spirit of God will surround and enfold you as you speak what you hear; astounding words of Wisdom and Power; the very oracles of God!

Day 8 - Have Faith

John 15:7
"If you abide in Me, and My words abide in you, you will ask what you desire, and it shall be done for you,"

Hebrews 11:33, 37 (NKJV)
33 "who through faith subdued kingdoms, worked righteousness, obtained promises, stopped the mouths of lions,
37 They were stoned, they were sawn in two, [k]were tempted, were slain with the sword. They wandered about in sheepskins and goatskins, being destitute, afflicted, tormented."

Active faith is a requirement for receiving from God. Answered prayer is perhaps the greatest faith building experience possible. How great to pray to Almighty God, and to have Him answer. This is God's plan, and it can happen to each and every child of God. But be not deceived, strong faith is costly. But when you are tried in the fire, you'll come out as pure gold.

(MSG :) vv 7-9; 12-13
7 Pure gold put in the fire comes out of it proved pure; genuine faith put through this suffering comes out proved genuine. When Jesus wraps this all up, it's your faith, not your gold, that God will have on display as evidence of his victory. 8 You never saw him, yet you love him. You still don't see him, yet you trust him - with laughter and singing. 9 Because you kept on believing, you'll get what you're looking forward to: total salvation.
12 Do you realize how fortunate you are? Angels would have given anything to be in on this! 13 So roll up your sleeves, put your mind in gear, be totally ready to receive the gift that's coming when Jesus arrives.

Beloved, you have the Spirit of Jesus Christ (with ALL of His power) within you, (as well as His love and nature). His power flows through you to bear much fruit. Jesus died to make this possible. Cling to His promises, allow His Words to give you the faith to ask and receive - MORE. Do not waste these benefits, be an "active doer" today, and not a hearer only. Being in Christ gives you the right to act on the Word in order to bear fruit in obedience to Jesus. For this purpose you have been sent! Faith is a mighty force that knows no defeat!

Day 9 - The Glory Cloud

2 Chronicles 5:13-14
"The trumpeters and singers joined in unison, as with one voice, to give praise and thanks to the Lord. Accompanied by trumpets, cymbals and other instruments, they raised their voices in praise to the Lord and sang: 'He is good: his love endures forever.' Then the temple of the Lord was filled with a cloud and the priests could not perform their service because of the cloud, for the glory of the Lord filled the temple of God."

Dear Ones, as the people of old entered into true worship, God's power was mightily released among them. God longs to demonstrate the (tangible) presence of His Power in your midst. He is the same God; He does not change. His power came in the form of a glory cloud that literally knocked the priests off their feet. Most times when the right atmosphere of worship is created, God's presence is brought down, then He inhabits the praises of His people and gladly tells them His secrets. He ministers back to you when you minister to Him in true praise and worship. His wonders are untold and His wisdom unsearchable.

Job gave a little description of Him in Job 26:7-14:
"He spreads out the northern skies over empty space, He suspends the earth over nothing, He wraps up the waters in His clouds, yet the clouds do not burst under their weight. He covers the face of the full moon, spreading His clouds over it. He marks out the horizon on the face of the waters for a boundary between light and darkness. The pillars of the heaven quake, aghast at His rebuke...And these are but the outer fringe of His works; how faint the whisper we hear of Him! Who can understand the thunder of His power?"

That is the greatness of the God who is calling for our worship. Do not hold back the tears, because tears accompany worship.

You may not be well known by the world but your love for the Master is unquestionable. You should hardly find a dry eye in the sanctuary or place of prayer and worship. As you behold His beauty against your unsightliness, you will most certainly break down in tears before Him. The worship that emanates from our hearts is an expression of how we truly feel towards God. It is to adore, admire, respect and venerate Him. He will come down and meet you in the form of His Shekinah Glory. How AWESOME! God is calling you to Worship! Worship until the tangible evidence of His presence come into your midst!

Day 10 – Do Not Let Wisdom Take A Back Seat

Ephesians 5:15 15-16 (NIV)
Be very careful, then, how you live—not as unwise but as
wise, 16 making the most of every opportunity, because the days
are evil.

James 1:5 (NIV)
If any of you lacks wisdom, you should ask God, who gives
generously to all without finding fault, and it will be given to
you.

Proverbs 9:10 (NIV)
The fear of the Lord is the beginning of wisdom, and knowledge
of the Holy One is understanding.

Do not let wisdom take a backseat. Let her rise up within you like the span and strength of an eagle's wings as he emerges from the valley of low esteem, poor performance and devaluation. Open your heart to seek the wisdom and knowledge woven in the very fabric of the astounding mystery of Godliness. You will inevitably experience the joy and the wonders that belongs to Christ alone...the awesome treasures that are locked within the vaults of heaven of heaven.

As you open your heart gate to the Holy Spirit, you will begin to ascend to the very pinnacle of the mind of Christ and your thoughts will give birth to new ideas and witty inventions. Rise from the dungeon of hopelessness, for a universe needing the forward thinking immersed in the secrecy of your thoughts; awaits for the sleeping giant to awaken.

Unlock the door to the endless possibilities that await you. You are powerful and awesome. Your capabilities are limitless and vast. Your God undergirds you and lifts your mind, soul and emotions far above that which could be reasonably owned or realized in the natural. By faith you have made a sizable investment and the initial step has already been made. Now is the time to make a withdrawal from the bank of wisdom. There are decisions to be made that will affect the entire world and you hold the keys. Your gift is not an ordinary one but extraordinary and framed with knowledge and understanding.

So, you need to get up front and personal with God today. Seek His Holy Will and His plan for your future. Spend a little more time in His presence and be filled with the *Fire* of God. You will find that the Power which God has planted within you will grow exponentially and you will have more wisdom than you've ever dreamed possible.

Day 11 - A New Beginning

Revelation 4:1
"After this I looked, and there before me was a door standing
open in Heaven. And the voice I had first heard speaking to me
like a trumpet said, "Come up here, and I will show you what
must take place after this."

This is a new beginning for many of us. It seems that so many
have been in a dry place; but know that the spiritual drought is
over! You can expect to see an increase in your spiritual gifts,
dreams, visions, and supernatural encounters. This will open the
opportunity for you to step up to a new level of ministry and see
the results of your efforts - which you have been long awaiting.

"For I will pour water on the thirsty land, and streams on the
dry ground; I will pour out My Spirit on your offspring, and My
blessing on your descendants." Isaiah 44:3

You will begin to experience a time of refreshing of God's Spirit.
This refreshing will be imparted upon all who are thirsty and all
who are weary. You will experience a restoration of the ministry
gifts that have been bestowed upon you; and you shall go forth
with greater power and assurance. In this season, you will begin
to step into the waters of Joel's Outpouring and many will come
to experience a deep renewal and fiery burning that cannot be
quenched by the storms of life. You will stride through the winds
and the waves of adversity with full assurance that God is indeed
with you and your deepest longing has been fulfilled. The fire
that burns within you shall be a perpetual fire that never goes
out. Your very countenance will changed as you are recharged
with the power of God.

The second part of this movement will be new rain from the
Holy Spirit, that will come upon those who are seeking all that
God has for them. Seek Him with your whole heart for He longs

to bless you. Many will be drawn into this great movement and many souls will be saved. In the midst of this, a new generation will begin to awaken to God's love, power, and acceptance; even the Joseph Generation. In every test of adversity, Joseph trusted God and found grace and prosperity. This next phase will bring God's power like we have never experienced it before. This will be a new level of God's fiery presence and healing. This is a start of a new healing movement with miracles, signs, wonders, and deeper revelation. Come and experience this new move.

Day 12 - Let God Solve Your Problems - Trust Him

Chronicles 20:17 NLT
"But you will not even need to fight. Take your positions; then stand still and watch the LORD's victory. He is with you, O people of Judah and Jerusalem. Do not be afraid or discouraged. Go out there tomorrow, for the LORD is with you!"

What God tells Jehoshaphat in this passage and what he would remind us of today is this: "The battle is not yours; it's mine. You don't have to fight in this battle." In other words, it's God's problem. Let Him solve it. The fact is, if you are God's child, then your problems are His problems. And He's much better at fighting your battles and solving your problems than you will ever be. Your job is to trust Him to work it all out. Perhaps the reason we have so many tired, fatigued, and discouraged Christians is because we think, "It all depends on me."

The day you resign as Assistant General Manager of the Universe, you're going to find that the world does not fall apart. You can relax in Faith, trusting that God is able to run things without your help. Twice in this passage He tells us, "Do not be afraid," and "do not be discouraged." When you face seemingly impossible situations, do not be afraid, and do not be discouraged. Has God ever lost a battle? Of course not! He always wins...He never loses. He just doesn't lose battles!

God told Jehoshaphat, "take your position and stand firm." What does it mean to stand firm? It means to have a mental attitude of quiet confidence. You stand firm on two things:

The Character of God:
He's Faithful - He does not bring us this far just to leave or let us down. He will not take you out on a limb and then cut the limb off. God is not schizophrenic! Believe in His Word. It is faithful, tried and true! Trust Him! Give Him your "all."

Let this be your secret prayer..."Father, I am overwhelmed by Your Love."
We love Him but yet we hold on to our hurts and wounds and minister to others from a wounded heart. Lord, I have given you everything else but this. But this time I lay it ALL down before you. My hurts; my fears; relationships; marriage; children; bad debts; anger; broken heart; wounded spirit; health; inabilities; guilt.

Exodus 33:14; 17
And He said, "My Presence will go with you, and I will give you rest."
So the Lord said to Moses, "I will also do this thing that you have spoken; for you have found grace in My sight, and I know you by name."

"Something good is coming your way!" You have been waiting on a blessing from on high! I am here to tell you that in a very short time, your blessing will come. God wants to give you a "New Normal." God takes pleasure in the prosperity of His servants. *The blessings of the Lord maketh rich! (Proverbs 10:22 - KJV)* He will withhold no good thing from you! Trust Him! He will bring it to pass.

Day 13 - This Is the Turning Point

Deut 2:1-2 (NASB)
"Then we turned and journeyed into the wilderness of the Way
of the Red Sea, as the Lord spoke to me, and we skirted Mount
Seir for many days. "And the Lord spoke to me, saying: You
have skirted this mountain long enough; turn northward."
'You have circled this mountain long enough!'

A Turning Point is a moment or season in time when a significant change takes place—one that leads to new and greater things.
In Deuteronomy, we learn of a time in which the children of Israel were doing a lot of 'turning", yet they were not making progress. They were not discovering new horizons. But that was set to change.

So let's look at the 'Big Picture." The Israelites had been traveling in the wilderness for 38 years. But in verse one (1), Moses describes it as 'many days'. A prophetic year is just as one day.
The day-year principle, year-day principle or year-for-a-day principle, is a method of interpretation of Bible prophecy in which the word day in prophecy is considered to be symbolic of a year of actual time. It is used principally by the historicist school of prophetic interpretation.

Yet, the bible says:

2 Peter 3:8 (KJV)
But, beloved, be not ignorant of this one thing, that one day is
with the Lord as a thousand years, and a thousand years as one
day.

Both for the short and the longer term, the nation had been stuck in a holding pattern. Anticipate areas that have frustrated you for a long period of time, being resolved.

As you come 'around the mountain' for the last time, you discover a horizon that wasn't available to you before. Trials of the past are bearing fruit. Your discernment and insight has been clarified and sharpened

And in during this period of time, in the very near future, Jesus will be the only explanation for what people may see taking place in and through you. This season shall be a Turning Point in the lives of many.

Day 14 - I Need A Little More Time; *Too Close Not To Receive The Victory Now!*

Joshua 10:12-13
12 On the day the Lord gave the Amorites over to Israel, Joshua said to the Lord in the presence of Israel:
"Sun, stand still over Gibeon, and you, moon, over the Valley of Aijalon."
13 So the sun stood still, and the moon stopped, till the nation avenged itself on its enemies, as it is written in the Book of Jashar.
The sun stopped in the middle of the sky and delayed going down about a full day.

Beloved, there is a link between time and purpose – time a purpose work together. "Lord, teach us to number our days that we may gain wisdom." (Teach me to stop wasting my time). Acquaint me and make me aware: Every day matters.

If you are going to fulfill your purpose, God has a window of opportunity for you to do so. Do not hesitate in doing those things that you have been called to do because there is an expiration date attached! Some people live a life of "que sera, sera" (what will be will be). But let me tell you that we were born on purpose; for a purpose. There is a reason that God chose us and a reason why we are still here! The devil wants you to believe to the contrary, but "you are somebody! You will survive the ups and downs in your life! Really, you will. You may feel like dying; but you are not your own, and God wants to do something in your life.

You can't keep living like you are living, because you were born for something else – this is not your ultimate; you were born for something else! Don't be afraid of that thing that has come against you. The Lord has given it into your hands. You are in control of it! Not the other way around. You are a winner!

When you are a winner and you lose, it affects you badly. When losers lose, it may not affect them badly, because they are losers anyway; they are comfortable with losing. A winner loses and his reputation is affected.

A fighter gets stronger in the middle of a fight. They find strength that they did not know they had. You don't know how strong you are until the attack comes on ("bring it on!!"). Come on Devil, "make my day!"

Day 15 - Traveling Mercies

Psalm 118:24 (NKJV)
This is the day the Lord has made; We will rejoice and be glad in it.

Father in the name of Jesus, we ask that you would impart your "peace" upon your people, your joy and most of all your love. We ask that Your Spirit would proceed us today on the highways, byways and airways. We pray that every mode of transportation would be safe and efficient. We thank you that every mode of transportation has been professionally and skillfully checked and serviced by knowledgeable mechanics and every part, screw, bolt, and instrument is functioning to its optimum capacity. We thank you that the second heaven is clear and all hindrances bound and inoperable.

We come against Principalities, Powers, Spiritual Wickedness in High Places and the Rulers of the Darkness of This World; we render them bound, helpless, hopeless and ineffective in all of their schemes and tactics, to hinder or delay your people from their preordained assignments. We thank you that Your angels are encamped around about them, and are holding them up in their hands, lest they should dash their foot upon a stone (calamity, hurt, harm, danger or distress). We bind every demonic chain and link representing incidents, accidents, every negative occurrence, and render them powerless in the Name of Jesus. We ask Father, that You would send forth Your warring angels to do battle for them in the heavenly realms, protect and uphold Your people against all opposing forces, in the name of Jesus. We thank you that they will be refreshed and emboldened when they reach their destinations. May Your divine will and purpose be accomplished today and every day, in the mighty name of Jesus - Amen.

Day 16 - Prayer for Missionaries

Isaiah 41:10 (NIV)
So do not fear, for I am with you; do not be dismayed, for I am your God. I will strengthen you and help you; I will uphold you with my righteous right hand.

Please continue to pray with me for our dear sisters and brothers who have unselfishly sacrificed their time, energy, love, resources and traveled far and wide (even to other continents), to share the "good news" of the gospel (and the awesome love of God), with those in need. We pray for restoration, peace, and the "rest" of God to abide with them today and always.

Father God, in the name of Jesus, we enter into Your throne room boldly and fearlessly, because of the access afforded to us by the Blood of the Lamb. We are sons and daughters, so we come before You reverently (and not stealthily), to find grace and help in our time of need. We thank You that Your mercies are new every morning and Your faithfulness is great towards us. We bring missionaries world-wide before you and pray that You would give them the grace, to show forth Your "likeness" before all men with humility. We thank you for our brothers and sisters who have sacrificed their time, energy, love, resources, and in many cases even their lives for the cause of Christ.

We pray that Restoration Power will begin to re-establish, mend, heal, repair and renew all godly relationships, in unity with the Spirit of God. By the Power of Your Holy Spirit and with the Sword of the Spirit, we come in collision with the hosts of hell and annihilate, destroy and extinguish their ungodly plans and devices sent forth to attack, harm and hinder the saints of God. We decree that missionaries will stand firm and function in the totality of their being, showing forth the Peace God among themselves and the people of God. We decree that they will be whole and complete in the perfection in which You have created them, in Jesus' name. By the power of Your   mighty Spirit and the working of Your will, we repair any broken threads and bonds of Love and Honor, woven together by the hand of the Spirit of God. Father, in the name of Jesus, we thank You for Your anointing upon missionaries, both locally and those called to the nations. We ask specifically for the safeguarding and continuation of the work that has been set upon each one, ordained and perfected by You, for we know that the anointing (of God) breaks the yokes of bondage.

We declare and decree, that they will be your hands extended to the people and that the people will "see Your face," as they worship and receive the word of God through your preachers, teachers, prophets, and conference speakers. Do it Lord, that your awesome Glory may be revealed among the people, in Jesus' matchless name, Amen.

Day 17 - No Turning Back

A Prayer For Those In The Service Of The Lord

1 Corinthians 10:13 (NIV)
No temptation has overtaken you except what is common to mankind.
And God is faithful; he will not let you be tempted beyond what you can bear. But when you are tempted, he will also provide a way out so that you can endure it.

Beloved, we have placed our hands on the plow and we cannot turn back now! Jesus said:

Luke 9:62
"No one who puts a hand to the plow and looks back is fit for service in the kingdom of God."

So, let us be strong and vigilant in our commitment to undergird our families, friends and loved ones and pray that God's watchful eye and hand of mercy will be upon them.
Please continue praying in your secret place and do touch and agree with our daily prayer as well.

Father, in the name of Jesus we come before you once again; we love You for who you are and not merely for the wonderful things that you have done (and continue to do), in our midst. We pray that Your grace and mercy will continue to be poured out upon Your people daily. Let them know that You have ordained them to do the work and equipped them with everything that they need to get the job done. Lord, we thank You that You have anointed them and appointed them to glorify Your Name in all the earth.

Cause them to know that the price is high but the reward is great. Let them know that they have not been chosen and appointed to a place of ease and tranquility of spirit, but rather to a place of great adversity and human need. Give them the courage and boldness not to shirk back, but to stand and encourage Your people, until You come with Holy Spirit Fire, to reveal Yourself to them in greater splendor and glory.

Father God, cause them to stand on Your word and strengthen their faith, that they may arise and believe, that indeed You have given them power over all the power of the enemy! Let them know and believe that new life shall result, when they call into existence, the mighty forces of Your power that will affect the everyday circumstances of Your people everywhere.

We declare and decree that this will become a "return investment," even unto their own lives; in the name of Jesus. Cause them to remember the word of God which is near (within) them, (even in their mouths, in their hearts and upon their lips), that they may know they shall decree a thing and You shall move to make it so. Father, show them Your Face, Your Power and Your Grace; that they may know and demonstrate among the people, the effectiveness of Your Grace that reveals, restores and brings miracles within their reach. Release the Fire, Lord. In the Mighty Name of Jesus - Amen.

Day 18 - Prepare For The Rain!

2 Corinthians 4:8-9
We are hard pressed on every side, but not crushed; perplexed, but not in despair; persecuted, but not abandoned; struck down, but not destroyed.

Father in the Name of Jesus we come into Your Holy Presence, with thanksgiving in our hearts. We thank You for dispersing the Rain of Your Holy Spirit upon Your people and making Your presence known, as You surround them with Your Love, Joy and Peace. We believe there is a river of life flowing in our hearts that when released, it will cause the lame to walk, the blind to see, the deaf to hear, needs will be met and many hearts turned to You.

We use our creative ability to call forth the Spirit of Unity among your ministers everywhere, which will release the Commanded Blessing from on high, in their midst. We come against all hindrances, closed doors and stumbling blocks, in the Name of Jesus.

We bind Principalities, Powers, Spiritual Wickedness In High Places, and Rulers of the Darkness of this world. We stand strong in the power of the Holy Ghost and the Blood of Jesus; and we bind these forces and render them powerless in the Mighty Name of Jesus. Satan, we serve you notice that your hindering tactics will not work. We cut off your power supply to all lower ranking demons and loose you from your bloodthirsty assignments against God's people.

Father we petition heaven to release a deluge of Your cleansing, purifying and sanctifying rain; open the floodgates of heaven that Your weary, torn and tattered people may witness life-changing miracles, signs and wonders, in the Name of Jesus. Lord send a deluge so great, that the roaring waters thereof will produce a thunderous sound that will shake even the netherworld, as You demonstrate Your power. This shaking shall cause chains to break, links to loosen and fall off, closed doors to open, mountains to fall, ropes to break and unravel, and walls to crumble. We speak Deliverance and Restoration, in the Name of Jesus! Let It Rain! Amen.

Day 19 - My Help

Psalm 121 (KJV)
I will lift up mine eyes unto the hills, from whence cometh my help.
He will not suffer thy foot to be moved: he that keepeth thee will not slumber. Behold, he that keepeth Israel shall neither slumber nor sleep.
The Lord is thy keeper: the Lord is thy shade upon thy right hand.
The sun shall not smite thee by day, nor the moon by night.
The Lord shall preserve thee from all evil: he shall preserve thy soul.
The Lord shall preserve thy going out and thy coming in from this time forth, and even for evermore.

Beloved, we have great potential to do greater things for God, but many times, our eyesight is limited and we only see the problem, not the solution. Let us fix our eyes firmly upon Jesus and not look to the right or left; for He alone has the power to save, deliver and make whole. Our confidence is totally in Him; for He is the "Promise Keeper." He will do, just what He said He would do. So stand tall in the spirit of unity; with one heart and one voice, give Him a glorious round of praise for what you are about to witness in your midst!

This is only the beginning; there is so much more to come! Be prepared to release the Unity of our Faith over your family, friends and loved ones, and also to the household of faith. You have longed for the Substance, (the witness of a tangible manifestation of your faith). But now, prepare yourselves in the Spirit of Unity (on one accord), and get ready to experience (and see with Spirit eyes), the Evidence (the outward sign of God's Glory in your presence)!!

Father, yet again, in the name of Jesus we come boldly to your throne. We lift up our families, friends and loved ones and especially those of the household of faith. We, like the Prophet Isaiah, are "undone' in your Holy presence. You are magnificent, glorious, omnipotent, omnipresent and omniscient. We worship and adore you Lord! You are a great and a mighty God. You are Alpha and Omega, and we love You Lord. There is no God like you! Lord, we ask that You would hear the heart-cry of Your people in this hour, that they may be empowered to recognize the inner beauty that You have created in them; that they may be confident in Your Love and Your ability to supply their every need, according to Your inexhaustible riches in glory by Christ Jesus. Let them know that it is never too late to pursue their dreams.

Father, we thank You that You have called us to be workers in Your vineyard. Though the workers may be few, cause us to know that we are mighty through the working of Your great power to heal the sick, set the captives free and deliver the oppressed from the yoke of bondage! Use us for Your glory Lord, and cause us to stand strong like (Gideon's army), against the forces of darkness; fully confident in knowing that the battle has already been won and You have given us the city! Open the eyes of our hearts that we may see and know You in all of Your splendor and magnificent glory.

We thank You for Your divine protection over our loved ones. Father, we are confident that those who come against them to do them harm, shall be as nothing. We stand in agreement with your word of power, strength, assurance, and confidence, that You will protect Your servants from the forces of evil, and pour out Your blessings upon each of us, as we endeavor to accomplish the work that You have assigned us to do. In the name of Jesus, we bind Principalities, Powers, Spiritual Wickedness in High Places, and Rulers of the Darkness of this World and render them unsuccessful in their attempts to do harm. Cause Your children to know that the enemy's forces are hopeless, ineffective and out-numbered exponentially, because a heavenly host of angel forces are with them this day to fight their battles.

We pray that a river of revelation would be poured out upon those in leadership. We ask You to raise up pastors, teachers, evangelists, apostles and prophets in this hour for the work of the ministry and the edification of the body of Christ. They will stand fearlessly before the enemy and let him know that enough is enough! Cause them to put on the whole armor of God, and Stand against the wiles of the devil, fully dressed and ready for battle; having put on the breastplate of righteousness, their feet shod with the preparation of the gospel of peace; and above all, taking the shield of faith that they may be able to quench all the fiery darts of the wicked.

Grant that they may take up and put on (by the working of Your Holy Will), the helmet of salvation, and the sword of the Spirit, which is the Word of God; that they may through prayer and supplication in the Spirit; watch with all perseverance for the saints, (in every city, town province and nation). (Ephesians 6:10-18 *paraphrased*)
We pray that there may be Unity and Vision between them all, in Jesus Name--Amen.

1 John 5:14-15 (NKJV)
Now this is the confidence that we have in Him, that if we ask anything according to His will, He hears us.
And if we know that He hears us, whatever we ask, we know that we have the petitions that we have asked of Him.

Day 20 - Dump and Pump!

Psalm 12:5
"Because the poor are plundered and the needy groan, I will now arise," says the LORD. "I will protect them from those who malign them."

Philippians 1:3
I thank my God upon every remembrance of you."

Beloved, I trust and pray that you are well and that Our Great and Mighty Father is revealing Himself to you (and most especially, those to whom you are sent and those for whom you stand in the gap) all the more as the days go by. We Bless the Lord for what He is doing in your midst!

A message to the Saints (around the world: -- Time is moving; and things are constantly changing. We are finding ourselves "overloaded" physically; financially; emotionally; relation-ally; and mentally. In fact, things are getting so bad, that you can't even remember the last time you've felt refreshed!

You are <u>always</u> encountering pressure on every level; your desires and needs are <u>always</u> overlooked. You're the wife, the mother, the caregiver, driver, chief cook and bottle-washer, secretary, the breadwinner and project manager! Everything to everybody! Well, everything must change and today marks the beginning of a turnaround in your lives.

You must dump the overload! Cast your cares upon Him, for He cares for you (1 Peter 5:9). Allow Holy Spirit to carry it. But first, you must "dump" (your burdens and excess baggage upon Him; and in return, He will "pump" (His refreshing waters into your weary, overloaded soul). This may not seem like a fair exchange but this is simply God's Favor! So let us learn this catchy phrase and simply refer to it as the: "Dump & Pump" Encounter! Most

Holy and Magnificent God Our Father, we come to You once again, in the Mighty Name of Jesus. We know that there is no other name whereby men can be saved, so we highly reverence His Immutable and Holy Name.

Lord, there is something about the name ....JESUS! Something happens in the atmosphere when we call upon His name. There is wonder-working power in His Name. Demons tremble when we call His Name...JESUS. So we lift our voices in Unity and Shout with a loud resounding voice (so as to cause the Jericho Walls of our "Overload" to fall in) J-E-S-U-S!!! Lord, we thank you! Come

Holy Spirit, we need You! We feel Your Presence Lord....Your Presence is with us now; to unload (our burdens) and to download Your love, joy and peace; Your cool refreshing waters. Father, You are the Potter; place us on Your wheel again...mold us, make us, extend us, expand us O Lord. We are ready for the change. We want to be just what You have designed us and desired us to be, in the name of Jesus. Pour out Your Refreshing upon Your people; upon the nations, let Your healing waters saturate their souls. Rain in the hearts of individuals. Breathe on them... "Breath of Life." Cause them to experience a surge of brand new life within their inner being. Quench every dry and thirsty soul; comfort every longing. Let the Soaking begin...Cause Your people to soak in the cleansing waters of Your Spirit....

Soak Beloved. Be drenched in His Presence. Experience the Anointing that will drown the Overload and Pump it out of the pipeline of your spirit. Soak...in the name of Jesus! Lord Jesus we thank You that You "led captivity captive and gave gifts to men" (Eph. 4:8). We are triumphant in You..... Amen!

Day 21 - The Blessings Of The Lord Are Upon You!

Psalm 112 (NIV) - declares a blessing upon you:
Praise the Lord. *Blessed* *are those who fear the Lord, who find*
great delight in His commands.
Their children will be mighty in the land; the generation of the
upright will be blessed. Wealth and riches are in their houses,
and their righteousness endures forever.
Even in darkness light dawns for the upright, for those who are
gracious and compassionate and righteous.

I want to speak a word of encouragement to the people of God today. The Lord has declared that he will pour out a blessing that you will not have room enough to receive. A blessing that will extend down through the generations! He just keeps pouring, and pouring, and pouring, and pouring.....Until there is no room left!! "Bless the generation of the upright. Wealth and riches shall be in their house."

There is a blessing awaiting if you just hold on! A blessing for our children and our children's children! To generations yet unborn! If you believe it then Praise God for it! No matter what you may be going through; do not allow the enemy to steal your Praise!

Father in the name of Jesus, make Your deeds known among the people today. Cause them to know that no matter how things may look, there is Purpose in this battle! We pray that You will give them the strength to endure and the courage to believe that there is a link between time and purpose.

We stand in the Spirit of Unity and decree that it is time for the people to truly believe Your word....and then act on it! Father, let them know that the race is not to the swift, nor the battle to the strong, but to them that endure until the end. Boldly we confess today, that each of us was born on purpose; - for a purpose! There is a reason that God chose us and a reason why we are still here! We say to the people of God:

"In the name of Jesus, you are somebody! The Devil may have wanted to abort you but God said no! I have a plan and purpose for his/her life. Death wants to take you away! But Gods says No! I have a Purpose and a Plan that yet needs to be fulfilled!"

Father, we thank You that Your people are not afraid of that thing that has come against them today, because You have heard their prayers and You Father, have given that for which they sought You, into their hands. You are in control of it! You are concerned with everything that concerns them! Cause them to know that now is not the time to give up, but rather to stay in the race.

You have sent out Your Special Forces! (Warring Angels), that excel in strength! Cause the people to know, trust and believe that You will contend with those who contend with them! We thank You Father that you are about to "Show Up, and Pour Out" a mighty Blessing upon Your people; the likes of which they have never known. And this Blessing shall be for them and their children, their children's children; even to generations yet unborn, in Jesus' name... Amen!

Day 22 - Do You Know Who Your Friends Are?

Proverbs 22:24-25 (NIV)
Do not make friends with a hot-tempered person, do not associate
with one easily angered, or you may <u>learn their ways </u> and get yourself ensnared.

Beloved, your friends matter to God. Have you ever thought to pray, "Lord, are my friendships pleasing to you?" A righteous friend can provide a link to the blessings and favor of God, because that individual encourages you toward a godly lifestyle. On the other hand, an unrighteous friend can be a binding chain to every kind of evil, leading you into terrible bondage. You probably have various circles of friends. You have a business circle (which includes your coworkers, partners or clients); a social circle (those whom you may associate with on a surface level); and you may also have contact with ungodly acquaintances. The apostle Paul says, it's impossible for us to avoid these kinds of contacts, otherwise we'd have to leave the world altogether!

The circle of friends God cares about most is your intimate circle, your bosom pals (if you will). These are the people you love most, and who have the most "influence" in your life. You are naturally attracted to one another, and you agree on most things; so you feel safe opening your heart to each other. In other words, you have an "affinity" with one another. Beloved, did you know that your hearts are constantly sending out signals; messages that attract others, to what is deepest within you? Please be careful to let the people know, that the devil is still on the prowl; and he wants them to form "ungodly soul ties" with those who say that they love God, but their hearts are far from Him. The enemy wants them to form friendships that will turn their hearts away from God, and back to the unresolved issues of the inner-man; to habits that they were never fully delivered from. Warn them!

Father God, in the name of Jesus, we come boldly to your throne today, seeking help that only you can give. We reverence and adore You, because You are the only wise and true God; an awesome wonder, mighty in all your ways! We thank You for Your Presence among us, and for revealing more of Your glory each day. We thank you for Your great Love for us and the people of the earth. We thank You that the "Best is Yet to Come!" We ask that You would Release Your Mighty Power upon Your people today in a special and unique manner. Send forth Your warring angels to <u>Release</u> the answers to prayers previously prayed and cause awesome testimonies of Your goodness and Mercy to come forth!

We speak to Principalities, Powers, Spiritual Wickedness in High Places, Rulers of the Darkness of this World; and declare that they are bound and inoperable, in Jesus' name! We cut off their power supply to all lower-ranking demons and loose them from their assignments of menacing the people of God, and trying to prevent them from coming into the fullness of God's blessings over their lives. We bind every ancestral curse and every ungodly soul tie in the name of Jesus Christ of Nazareth!

We remind you Satan, that you are a defeated foe; Jesus defeated you at Calvary, triumphed over you and made an open show of You! We have been given power over you and remind you that you are under our feet! We command you to come out, detach yourself from all who are bound, and go where Jesus sends you, until He places you in eternal chains. Father we close every door of sickness, poverty, lack, confusion, broken promises, broken hearts, and broken spirits in the name of Jesus! We ask You to seal them with the blood of Jesus and prevent re-entry!

Cause a mighty Break-through, Break-open, and Break-out to occur among the people! We pray that You would Loose the Bonds of Wickedness in their lives, and the lives of their descendants; in the mighty name of Jesus! Let them shout with a loud voice, "I'm Free; Hallelujah, I'm Free!" Lord, open their eyes to all of their friendships! Help the people to clearly see and discern true friendships, whether they are good or bad, pleasing or not pleasing to You. May all of their friendships bring glory to You! Restore and bring forth Godly Relationships, in the name of Jesus.....Amen!

Day 23 - Go Out There Tomorrow; the Lord Is

With You

Psalms 37:4 (KJV)
Delight thyself also in the LORD; and he shall give thee the
desires of thine heart.

John 9:4 (NLT)
"We must quickly carry out the tasks assigned us by the one
who sent us. The night is coming, and then no one can work."
(John 9:4 NLT).

Dear Ones, Time waits for no one. It is possible, that you now have more time behind you than you have ahead. There is still so much to do. I believe the Lord is well pleased with what you have accomplished. You must be pretty tired by now, but you have only to look to the Lord and He will restore, refill, refresh and replenish you for the completion of the task. Beloved, at some point, we all must simply turn all of our concerns over to Jesus and trust Him to sort out (with great distinction), those things that have been accomplished (according to His holy will) and what yet remains. He promised to be with you until the very end.

"But you will not even need to fight. Take your positions; then stand still and watch the LORD's victory.
He is with you, O people of Judah and Jerusalem. Do not be afraid or discouraged.
Go out there tomorrow, for the LORD is with you!"
(2 Chronicles 20:17 NLT).

Father, in the name of Jesus, we come before you, lifting up those of the household of faith who make their boast in you. "God is our strength, our provider, our hiding place, our strong tower, our protector, our deliverer all the day long. We must

217

now show the world that the God we serve will do all that He promised.....and more!" Father we thank You for the Holy Spirit who walks alongside them to strengthen and keep them. You are their shield and their buckler Lord, Your Word is being fulfilled quickly in this hour; everything is being shaken, exactly as they were warned. Cause your saints to know that this is the day of Your Power.

Father, by Your Spirit that is at work in them, let them know that You will lift up their heads and comfort them when they tire; You will cause them to walk in even greater divine authority. Cause them to hear Your still small, still voice, as You call them to Yourself, to tell them that they are experiencing Your presence in a different way; for these are the days of the revealing of Your Glory. Father, in Jesus' name, we continue to thank You for allowing them to "Walk it Out and be amazed, as You Work Out every detail for Your Glory.

Lord, we stand amazed that in this hour, You are honoring prophetic promises that were previously made; of which your people perhaps, have experienced a form of fulfillment that was less than what You intended; and have settled for less than the best. We ask that for their faithfulness, You would fulfill Your whole promise to them.

Break the spirit of barrenness off their lives and their ministries; so that they may produce ALL that You have called them to walk in. Cause them to experience Your Kingdom (on earth), as their praises touch the realms of glory. Let their worship merge with all that is holy and powerful....in Jesus' Mighty Name.......Amen.

Day 24 - Victory in Jesus!

Psalm 91
1 Whoever dwells in the shelter of the Most High will rest in the shadow of the Almighty. 2 I will say of the LORD, "He is my refuge and my fortress, my God, in whom I trust."
3 Surely he will save you from the fowler's snare and from the deadly pestilence. 4 He will cover you with his feathers, and under his wings you will find refuge; his faithfulness will be your shield and rampart. 5 You will not fear the terror of night, nor the arrow that flies by day, 6 nor the pestilence that stalks in the darkness, nor the plague that destroys at midday. 7 A thousand may fall at your side, ten thousand at your right hand, but it will not come near you. 8 You will only observe with your eyes and see the punishment of the wicked. 9 If you say, "The LORD is my refuge," and you make the Most High your dwelling, 10 no harm will overtake you, no disaster will come near your tent. 11 For he will command his angels concerning you to guard you in all your ways; 12 they will lift you up in their hands, so that you will not strike your foot against a stone. 13 You will tread on the lion and the cobra; you will trample the great lion and the serpent. 14 "Because he loves me," says the LORD, "I will rescue him; I will protect him, for he acknowledges my name. 15 He will call on me, and I will answer him; I will be with him in trouble, I will deliver him and honor him. 16 With long life I will satisfy him and show him my salvation."

Beloved, have you ever been called to something too big for you to put on? Have you ever been up front and confused? Ever had to lead and did not know which way to go? Often in ministry, we need to be up front and honest with people. We need to tell them, "If you are going to follow me, you need to hang in there with me, because I just don't know. I do know that God has called me and we are going somewhere, but the details, I simply cannot tell you. I can only trust God's leading.

219

I also know that sometimes, when people think they are there; they stop thinking; praying; and laying prostrate before God. They sometimes look to those of us who are in ministry, as though we do not experience and go through the struggles, tests and trials that they do. Often, what we think is a good idea, is not what God has for us. We need to learn to listen to His voice and then, wait patiently on Him! Hang out in His Presence a while. He is able to keep that which we have committed unto Him. He protects us, provides for us and makes His will known, when the "me" in us gets the notion that it is right. It's not about what you think.

Father, in the name of Jesus, we come before You, seeking Your face and asking for Your divine direction for our lives and the lives of those whom You have sent us. We thank You that Your mercies are new every morning and Your faithfulness is great towards us. We are thankful that You are concerned with those things that concern us. We ask that You would hide us in Your Holiness and surround us with your goodness, and Your loving-kindness. Make known to us the Mystery of Your will, according to your good pleasure. You are a Great and Mighty God, who has gone before us to bless us in a special way. We have witnessed your power, grace and mercy. We believe that there is yet more to come.

Father, You have given us the power and boldness to share your word in season to those who so readily receive it. For it was You who said, "He who receives you, receives Me; and he who receives Me receives Him who sent Me." (Mt. 10:40). Thank You Father, for the new mercies and bountiful blessings that You have poured out upon Your people. Thank You for the mighty change that You are about to bring forth over this nation. It is time for Your people to quit living in the land of Bondage, and start living in the land of milk and honey!

Let Your people know that You have heard their prayers and supplications which they have placed before You; and now it is time that they should look to heaven and expect a response. Now it is even time for the reward! In the Name of Jesus; Healing, Victory, Prosperity, Deliverance, Love, Joy, Peace belongs to them! Lord, cause the people to Rejoice; and bring forth a resounding Shout of Praise!! For You have already provided! Let them cry VICTORY!! For what the Lord has done in their midst! In the name of Jesus.......Amen!

Day 25 - Forging Ahead

Romans 16:19-20 (NIV)
Everyone has heard about your obedience, so I rejoice because of you; but I want you to be wise about what is good, and innocent about what is evil. The God of peace will soon crush Satan under your feet. The grace of our Lord Jesus be with you.

In our daily interactions with people, we will meet some who are nice and some who are downright mean to us. Due to our fallen human nature, we tend to replay in our minds the nasty incidents and hurtful words we encounter in our relationships. We become distracted by the voices of these unpleasant people. Instead of dwelling on these negative voices and letting other people define who we are, what is the voice of God (spoken through His Word), saying about us? Does God think you are unnecessarily fearful? Definitely not, because He says you are fearfully and wonderfully made (Psalm 139:14). Did He make you like the people you know? Of course not. He has wired you differently because He is a God of variety:

1 Corinthians 12:4-6 (NIV)
"There are different kinds of gifts, but the same Spirit distributes them. There are different kinds of service, but the same Lord. There are different kinds of working, but in all of them and in everyone it is the same God at work."

For example, He may have made you to be more quiet and introverted. Being so, you may, in front of certain significant people (whom perhaps, you think don't like you), prefer to be quiet rather than expose yourself to criticisms from them. As such, you become overly conscious of people's opinion of you. Such powerful feelings of self-consciousness cannot merely be willed away. Instead, when you turn to God and ask Him to help you, God will go through these encounters with you; both the pleasant and the unpleasant. Through those very encounters, God will strengthen your inner being so that the sting from the unfair comments, become less painful even though they are still there. Actually, sometimes we must let go of past situations and people. What that time comes, just simply, scroll, select and delete!

Philippians 3:13 (KJV)
"Brethren, I do not count myself to have apprehended; but one thing I do, forgetting those things which are behind and reaching forward to those things which are ahead,"

Father God, we come before you now, in the name of Jesus. We thank You that You are always with us, in every step that we take and every turn that we make. Through it all, we've learned to trust You more, to love you more dearly, more deeply, and to experience Your love more completely. WE ask You to fill our cups each day, with just what we need to carry out Your Divine Will; no less or no more. Do it Lord for Your Glory, that we may with one voice, testify of the great things that You have done in our midst and make Your name famous on the earth!

Malachi 1:11 (NIV)
My name will be great among the nations, from where the sun rises to where it sets. In every place incense and pure offerings will be brought to me, because my name will be great among the nations," says the LORD Almighty.

Father, we thank you that we have answered the call and extended our "Hands of Love" freely, (selflessly) to those in need. We thank You that we abide under the covering of the blood of Jesus and the prayer of intercession. We declare and decree that spirits of "lone ranger," rebellion, mutiny, cliques, and false prophetic unction will not come among us and cause division. We pray that the spirits of unity, cohesiveness, apostolic vision, prophetic insight, and holiness will be released among Your servants, in the name of Jesus. Father, we thank You that we will make up the hedge and build walls around the body of Christ in these last days. In Jesus' Mighty Name - Amen!!

Day 26 - Obedience

Hebrews 5:8 (KJV)
Though he were a Son, yet learned he obedience by the things which he suffered.

1 Samuel 15:22 (KJV)
And Samuel said, Hath the Lord as great delight in burnt offerings and sacrifices, as in obeying the voice of the Lord? Behold, to obey is better than sacrifice, and to hearken than the fat of rams.

Beloved, when your heart is open to obey My word, and your ear open to hear the voice of My Spirit, I am free to fill your life with the abundance of My grace.

To The Servants of the Lord in the Mission Fields

We have traveled with you (in the Spirit) to faraway places. Our hearts are joyful as we so graciously share in this wondrous work, that God has done through your love and compassion for the Nations. We are forever grateful to have been on this journey with you. Though your work is still not over, we wanted to take this time to let you know how much we appreciate you and your labor of "Love.".

Father, in the name of Jesus we ask that you bless and keep your children. Let this time of giving, receiving and pouring-out be a "Forever Experience" for them. Cause them to forever treasure the outpouring of Your grace, mercy and lovingkindness in their midst. May Your Word be forever etched upon the tablets of their hearts. May their memories be forever flooded, with the many times You reached down from heaven, touched their deepest yearning and quenched their thirsty souls. May they be kept forever in Your care.

Father, we pray that they may forever remember how You supplied every need (right on time), gave them courage to run through troops and leap over walls, caused them to accomplish the tasks assigned and soar to the next level of their purpose. Let them know Father, that they will walk in the strength of this experience forever; in the name of Jesus......Amen.

Day 27 - To Those Who Prayed

2 Timothy 4:7 (NKJV)
I have fought the good fight, I have finished the race, I have kept the faith.

We thank God, Our Father for your support and fellowship in the Spirit of Unity. We know that the Blanket of Praise has been spread for those who received and experienced the awesome healings and breakthroughs that Our Father sent in answer to your prayers. Some have indeed received a mighty outpouring of God's infinite grace and mercy upon their lives, and those of their loved ones, all because of your great sacrifice and labor of love.

Father, we pray for the safety of Your saints. May they be blessed when they go out and when they come in. We pray a 30-60-100 fold return on the seed that they have sewn in the kingdom. We ask You to enfold Your saints, cover them and hold them close to Your breast (for You are the Mighty Breasted One); that they may actually feel and display (according to Ephesians 3:18) both spiritually and physically, the dimensions of Your love, every day for the rest of their lives.

We ask that You would go before them today (and every day); make straight the crooked path, and make the rough terrain totally passable. Bless them and their households (for generations to come). In the name of Jesus...Amen!

Let everything that has breath *PRAISE HIS HOLY NAME*!! Praise the Lord for the "great things" He has done!

Day 28 - Saving the Best for Last

John 2:1-11
On the third day there was a wedding in Cana of Galilee, and the mother of Jesus was there; 2 and both Jesus and His disciples were invited to the wedding. 3 When the wine ran out, the mother of Jesus *said to Him, "They have no wine." 4 And Jesus *said to her, "Woman, what does that have to do with us? My hour has not yet come." 5 His mother *said to the servants, "Whatever He says to you, do it." 6 Now there were six stone waterpots set there for the Jewish custom of purification, containing twenty or thirty gallons each. 7 Jesus *said to them, "Fill the waterpots with water." So they filled them up to the brim. 8 And He *said to them, "Draw some out now and take it to the [c]headwaiter." So they took it to him. 9 When the headwaiter tasted the water which had become wine, and did not know where it came from (but the servants who had drawn the water knew), the headwaiter *called the bridegroom, 10 and *said to him, "Every man serves the good wine first, and when the people have drunk freely, then he serves the poorer wine; but you have kept the good wine until now." 11 This beginning of His signs Jesus did in Cana of Galilee, and manifested His glory, and His disciples believed in Him.

Beloved, a songwriter once said:
"Now the day is over, night is drawing nigh,
Shadows of the evening steal across the sky."
Unknown

We are closer to our Lord's return than ever before in history. Often in the hustle and bustle of our daily work, we do not always remember to see the beauty of God's creation, or notice the form of a snowflake, or watch the pattern of the rain as it skips upon the gray and dusty terrain. Are we so engrossed with our own thoughts and feelings that we fail to see the big picture that God painted on the canvas of the universe? He has paid attention to every detail of our inheritance. He has carefully prepared a place for us in His Kingdom and when He returns, (as heirs, kings and priests), we shall reign and rule with Him there! It shall be a Far Better Place; a Holy Place. Like nothing ever seen before! Jesus said:

John 14 – The Message (MSG)
1-4 There is plenty of room for you in my Father's home. If that weren't so, would I have told you that I'm on my way to get a room ready for you? And if I'm on my way to get your room ready, I'll come back and get you so you can live where I live. And you already know the road I'm taking."

18-20 "I will not leave you orphaned. I'm coming back. In just a little while the world will no longer see me, but you're going to see me because I am alive and you're about to come alive. At that moment you will know absolutely that I'm in my Father, and you're in me, and I'm in you.

29-31 "I've told you this ahead of time, before it happens, so that when it does happen, the confirmation will deepen your belief in me. I'll not be talking with you much more like this because the chief of this godless world is about to attack. But don't worry— he has nothing on me, no claim on me. But so the world might know how thoroughly I love the Father, I am carrying out my Father's instructions right down to the last detail.
"Get up. Let's go. It's time to leave here."

1 Thessalonians 4:16-17 (KJV)
16 For the Lord himself shall descend from heaven with a shout, with the voice of the archangel, and with the trump of God: and the dead in Christ shall rise first:
17 Then we which are alive and remain shall be caught up together with them in the clouds, to meet the Lord in the air: and so shall we ever be with the Lord.

Jeremiah 29:11-13
For I know the thoughts that I think toward you, saith the Lord, thoughts of peace, and not of evil, to give you an expected end. (Hope in your final outcome)
Then shall ye call upon me, and ye shall go and pray unto me, and I will hearken unto you. And ye shall seek me, and find me, when ye search for me, with all your heart.

Jeremiah 51:15
He hath, made the earth by His power; He hath established the world by His wisdom, and hath stretched out the heaven by his understanding.